Dying to Self

TASHERA SIMMONS

For permission requests, write to the publisher, addressed "Attention: Permissions Coordinator," 205 N. Michigan Avenue, Suite #810, Chicago, IL 60601. 13th & Joan books may be purchased for educational, business or sales promotional use. For information, please email the Sales Department at sales@13thandjoan.com.

Printed in the U. S. A.

First Printing, March 2025

Library of Congress Cataloging-in-Publication Data has been applied for.

ISBN: 978-1-961863-85-9

dedication

I WANT TO DEDICATE this book to the broken child in me. She never got a chance to be the little girl she always dreamed to be in a healthy way. She should have had a chance to do so and transition into a healthy young woman. As long as I have breath in my body, it's never too late. To live my life to its fullest.

I am grateful I was able to die to myself and be a better version of me.

I want to give all my praises to the Almighty God for never leaving me nor forsaking me, for holding my hand every step of the way in life and never letting me go,

To my four amazing God-sent children: Xavier, Tacoma, Sean, and Praise, and my goddaughter Paige Hurd. My literal earth angels, I really thank you for showing me what unconditional love feels and looks like. In my darkest days, you all in your own special ways brought the sun to my heart, stability to my life, and peace and happiness in the storm.

Through your love, I was able to withstand every trick the devil threw at me. I am so grateful that I have the honor to do life with you all.

To my friends and family, thank you for loving me and supporting me through my ups and downs. I am so grateful to have a great support system. It never goes unnoticed. I love you all deeply.

Last but not least, to my hero, my father, who taught me what true selfless love looks like. You are one of the strongest warriors I have ever known, and one of the wisest men I've ever come across. You will forever be in my heart. I miss you every day. Rest in love, Daddy. We did it.

acknowledgements

A SPECIAL THANKS to my godmother Linda Robinson for stepping up into my life as a little lost girl and teaching me how to be a young, clean, respectable young woman in the second leg of life.

Thank you to all the humans who I have crossed paths with in a positive way. You literally changed my life and my perspective.

I want to thank my therapist of nine years, Judy Adamo, for not only changing my life but my perspective on how to move forward through my darkest days with dignity and love.

Thank you to my attorney of 10 years, Lita Rosario-Richardson, for showing me what a strong, stand-up, bad-ass bitch looks like and proving she can also be a kind caring loyal human being at the same time in an evil industry. I truly love you for that.

Shout out to all my childhood sister friends who continually sustain a firm foundation in my life! Love y'all for life!

A special thanks to my 13th & Joan Publishing team for your patience, dedication, amazing writing skills, and ability to capture my heart in every story. Thank you for believing in me and my story while guiding me through it all no matter how choppy the waters got. You stood 10 toes in with me till the end.

Thank you to my amazing, creative, and talented photographer, Auckvision, for perfectly capturing exactly what I envisioned for the book cover.

Thank you to my make-up artist, Star, for nailing my miserable make-up look for my book cover.

Thank you to my publicity team, April Love Publicity, for working diligently to get me out there and building my brand.

We are hurting because we are not allowing God to come in.

Tashera Simmons

contents

dear reader

AN OPEN LETTER TO THE LOST SOUL

I AM the ex-wife of Earl Simmons, the famous rapper and actor who performed as DMX before he returned to our Heavenly Father in 2021. I shared the story of our nearly 15 years of marriage and divorce in my first book, *You Think You Know, but You Have No Idea*, published in 2013. Readers were enthralled as I revealed details of our beautiful yet tumultuous relationship that began when we were just kids and evolved to include struggles of abuse, adultery, and drug addiction. The positivity of our relationship outweighed the tough situations but when disagreement ensued, it was a harsh reality in our lives.

In *Dying to Self*, I focus on the truth that people do not know how to be real. I, too, have struggled to speak my truth, especially when I was in my darkest places and lost. I didn't know if it was the right thing to do, as it seemed very unpopular. My hesitancy was also tied to the fact that I didn't know my worth. I didn't know who I was. I consequently only spoke honestly about my life and the feelings weighing heavy on my heart when I was with my closest circle or maybe one-on-one with a stranger. When I did speak the truth, I realized others were empowered.

I have learned that there are many things I can live without, which unfortunately is a truth many realize only after they have fallen knee-deep into the pool of trinkets and gadgets that they thought would bring happiness. But possessions and money can never make anyone happy. Only one thing can bring us the eternal joy we all have been looking for, and His name is God.

Without God in our lives, we allow the evils of this world to take hold and keep us forever in a place of no hope and despair. When we finally open our eyes to the one true King, our Lord and Savior, the pain and anger that once seemed inevitably intertwined with being a human will disappear and never return. Life does not have to be challenging but without God at the forefront of our minds and decisions, we can never overcome challenges.

My goal in *Dying to Self* is to help you understand that you no longer need to be lost. You no longer need to suffer. With God at the helm, you can live to fulfill your destiny. I encourage you to connect to God and the Holy Spirit, which requires dying to yourself every day to be the person God has called you to be.

introduction

Don't live by your flesh.
It will always fail you.

Tashera Simmons

PEOPLE ARE ALWAYS asking me, *"How did you get to this place? How are you able to give your whole heart to God?"* I tell them, this fleshy body that we live in is messed up. We may appear to look perfect on the outside, but inside we are fighting a battle. This is not a beautiful war but a mission for our souls. No one is perfect or will ever be. We all have our flaws and our downfalls. I do not think I'm perfect, not by a long shot. How was I able to get to this different level in life spiritually?

It started with allowing my spirit to connect with the source, which is God.

Connecting with God on a spiritual level is the most amazing experience you can have. I drew closer to him when I started to read the Bible, fast, and pray. You could have all the wealth and material things in the world, but all of it means nothing if you do not have your spirit right. We do not always function by allowing our spirit to guide us, which keeps us from growing.

We are so focused on what we can see with our natural eyes that we don't believe the unseen. The greatest trick the enemy has been able to pull off is making people think he doesn't exist. If we think we will never plant a garden, we won't. In the physical world, we don't seem to have a green thumb. We have read all the books and applied all the methods, but our plants always die. Once we open our word and begin to read, it becomes alive to us. Wisdom and knowledge are downloaded in our mind, and we find ourselves watering the plant differently. We have instincts on how to nourish the plant. That is what it is like being in the flesh versus the spirit. The flesh tells me I can't do it, and I have tried everything in my own strength. The spirit gives me what I need.

I have met some of the greatest people around the world. These are the people most would look up to because of the material things they possess. They come across as being super smart and well put together. The generations tend to idolize them. People plan how their day will be based on how this specific "influencer" lives their life. Others will buy the clothing they wear or the beverages they were seen drinking. We see the kind gestures they do for others on the television screen and the organizations they support. We soak it up and believe every word. We start to want to become what we see, not knowing we are only observing the individual from the outside and not their inner-being.

If we were created in transparency, we would be able to see what's on the inside, but we are not. We decipher something isn't quite right based on our spirit not sitting right. What does that mean? We feel antsy when a person is around. We can't understand why we are uncomfortable around them. There is something about them that bothers us, and it seems crazy. We don't understand it. We try to be in situations with them, but we can't stay long. It is because they have internal demons that no one sees and they hide well. In reality, it is eating them alive and preventing their true authentic self from breaking free.

Our flesh can hold us hostage to keeping those demons. Our belief system of doing the wrong things and hoping they become right cripples us. We can't hurt someone and expect others to not hurt us. This truth is revealed in Scripture: *So in everything, do to others what you would have them do to you, for this sums up the Law and the Prophets* (Matthew 7:12). When we focus on our body and live in our flesh, we make it okay to be wrong. We can easily become addicted to people, places, or things because our flesh lusts for it.

Flesh can have us eating sugary foods when we know we are diabetic or not working out when we are overweight. Flesh tells us it's okay to be unhealthy in our mind, body, and spirit. One day our flesh will fail us, so we have to die to our flesh. Our spirit keeps us away from those things that are harmful. When we are in touch with God in our spirit, we are led down the right path. We tend to frown upon certain things we used to like. We may no longer have a taste for alcohol or want to have sex outside of marriage. Our friends and family may think we are strange or "losing it" because we aren't the same person they have become used to, but it's okay. We are not that version of ourselves anymore.

We have learned to start living in our spirit, which is the best way to be. We have a peace that makes us smile everyday, even in pain, knowing everything will be alright. Our world is crumbling around us, but we are singing with the birds. Giving God our heart means turning our cares over to Him. We no longer stress over the "what if" because we know God can. The word "No" doesn't exist because with God, all things are possible (Matthew 19:26).

When it's time to leave this earth, our flesh will die but our spirit will live on. Our spirit makes us aware of trouble ahead and gives us the wisdom to stay away. It lets us know the right foods to eat by changing our palate. People tied to our destiny show up because we are in the right place at the right time, and they escort us into our purpose.

My spirit led me to write this book for you. I know the fight with flesh is a never-ending battle, but you have the victory. For so long I wanted to tell my story. People ask about why I choose God. The answer is, He chose me. From the day I was formed in my mother's womb, He had a plan for me. Even on my worst days, I knew I could depend on Him. When family and friends fail, He is always there for me.

I can give God my heart because He will never break it. I give Him my problems and He provides a solution. He has taken care of me my entire life, even before I had any idea of who He was. That is why I trust, love, and adore Him. As a parent, you can love your children and as a wife you can love your husband, but they will frustrate you. Soon enough you will not be happy with a decision they make, but you can't allow what they do to affect your love for God.

When I took the time and died to my flesh as well as how I felt things should happen, my spirit rose up. I was able to get through my toughest times with God on my side. I want to let you know the battle is the Lord's. My story is to help you understand we all go through trials and tribulation, but you are a winner in the end. I had to die to my ideas and wants. I had to realize, we are born for a bigger reason. No matter your income bracket or status, God loves you. I know I am a child of the most high God, and getting closer to Him has changed everything about me.

For each person who reads my book, I want you to know behind every great man there is a great woman. She goes through a process throughout her journey so she can achieve her purpose. We all have assignments and a mission led by God. Some we are aware of and some we are not. I urge you not to judge the stories my ex-husband was a part of. He was only a human being having a human experience, just like you and me. My situations were no better or worse than anyone else but ultimately, they took me to the highest place that God has called me to be.

We all go through tests and trials in life. Sometimes the challenges involve parenting, marriage, friendship, or even relatives. My point is it's all designed so we can reach the highest, best version of ourselves. We're either going to win or lose, and the choice is ours! With that said, sit back, relax, and enjoy your new read.

chapter i

BETRAYAL

No matter how much the spirit of
betrayal just wanted to sit on me,
I always managed to stay in the light.
Always.

Tashera Simmons

THE INTRO

BETRAYAL HAS BEEN a best friend to me—the type who stays close long enough to plot, scheme, and finally attempt to take you out as if it were the plan all along. My first love who became my husband, my father, and eventually my mother all betrayed me. My mother was the first to do it. Each time it happened, I greeted betrayal and allowed it to shake me and sway me, but it never had the power to rip me from solid ground.

You can see the signs of betrayal coming before it actually happens, but what do you do after it hits you dead in the face, knocking out all the fight you had left in you? I'll say this: The answer is not in revenge nor is it in bitterness. The answer lies in standing in the light.

THE STORY

AS A 10-YEAR-OLD GIRL in Yonkers, New York, I would often find myself coming to a still point just above the Hudson. The train was just entering the city. The chill air pricked the nape of my neck as my dad stood tall next to me. He pointed to the train and said some clever facts about the type of train it was, where it was headed, and the sound of the whistle or modern day air horn. I watched him closely. He was happy around me. He was my comfort. The sun was going down and we were in no hurry, yet we had someplace to be. Our daddy-daughter time at the jazz concert was something I always looked forward to and in moments like those, I let him talk all he wanted. He had my full attention. He taught me the importance of being a woman, how important gratitude and integrity are, and my worth when it came to men. When he finally had enough of his teaching and I had enough of listening, he looked at his watch.

"We better get going. Are you ready?" he asked.

"Always Daddy," I responded.

"All right! Let's go firstborn."

I hooked my little arm underneath his, and we made our way to the jazz concert.

For the next four years, my dad's words would continue to affirm me and brighten my world. By the time I was 14, my youngest brother was about 1 year old. I took my role as older sister seriously. One morning, I saw my mother pacing the living room. She had a worried look, and her face was wet. I had caught her teary-eyed on many occasions before, so I didn't even have to ask her what was the matter. She just shook her head.

"I'm okay, Tashera. I need you to make breakfast this morning for me. Will you do that?"

"Of course," I said, as she reached out and touched my face.

"Thank you. I can always count on you."

I went on and made breakfast for the house. Grits, toast, and what was left of the sausage. We shared a meal together. My youngest brother made such a mess out of the grits.

One day my mother went to the corner store and never came back. Vanished. She pulled off the Houdini act of the century, leaving seven kids behind. My dad was so hurt, and I felt like I constantly had a pit in my stomach. This was the very first betrayal, and I will never forget how it shook our family and affected my relationships moving forward.

Some time had passed after my mother dissolved from my life before I began to notice a shift in my dad's treatment toward me. It was like day and night. He said that I looked so much like her and that I was going to be nothing. He became very verbally and emotionally abusive in the worst way. I would do everything in my might to hold onto all the good things he used to say, but those memories began to fade away as his verbiage became demeaning. This shift in itself was a betrayal.

The notion of betrayal is often linked with a sense of trust that has been violently broken. For 14 years, I trusted my dad to be my protector and to never turn on me like he did. I was still dealing with the betrayal of my mother, so to add him on top of everything was almost suffocating. I was so young. When you're young and trauma hits, it's not the same as when you're an adult. Maybe that's because your mind is still being molded and formed and you're having all these different new emotions. I believe I was very numb to that betrayal but also very devastated and lost.

I met the love of my life at the age of 11. Earl, he was the one. We officially got together when I was 17. I remember he had a reputation of just living this free life. He did what he wanted, and that was attractive to me. He too was betrayed and never really had a mother or a father. He wanted to be to me what he never had. He saw in me the mother and nurturing that he never got from his mom. In return, he had a protective nature and masculinity that made him stronger, even though I was dominant. He really gave me what I was missing from my dad at that point in life.

Earl and I began to build a life together over the next 35 years so when he betrayed me for the first time, it truly hit differently because we were cut from the same cloth. We shared that same feeling of abandonment and betrayal from the people we loved the most. We both knew what it was like, so there were many nights where we would just let out some of the things from our past. We'd both be crying. We had this understanding where we would never do those same hurtful things to each other, especially after creating a family of our own. We really communicated about how we would never let that old friend betrayal through our front door.

Living with Earl, I felt a sense of déjà vu. I was reliving the foundation of a family that my parents built that had many cracks in it. This was a strange feeling. It almost felt as if those cracks were being mended back together, and I had a second chance to leave betrayal behind with a new love and a new family. Like I said before, you can see the signs of betrayal before it comes. Each time it came, I had to heal in a new way.

The last time I was betrayed—and it shall remain the very last time—was by Earl's then girlfriend. Earl and I were still married but had been estranged for around eight years. He ended up giving her a ring like he did with many other women. I saw so much of myself in this girl. I took her in like a stray and really began to care for her. Earl was not the man I had once loved. The physical and verbal abuse was absolutely horrible to this young lady. I felt as if he attracted people based on how he felt about himself. He didn't feel good about himself, so he had people around him who didn't feel good about themselves.

We were no longer together, but we had a bond that kept us close as friends. As I moved on from him, I found myself again and ultimately, I began radiating this light. When he came around me, my light was so bright it was almost to the point where I reminded him of what he left and lost. This would make him feel sad. I could see it in his eyes and demeanor.

"Why are you so depressed? Why is your spirit so down?" I would ask him.

Not much of an answer came out of his lips, but to my surprise, an apology.

"I'm so sorry for everything," he said to me. "You didn't deserve nothing that I did to you."

I felt uncomfortable when he said this, which was also surprising because all I ever wanted from him was an apology. Something had shifted in him. He would get his girlfriend to call me up sometimes and would encourage me to take her under my wing. I took a liking to her and did what I could to minister to her and build her up. In an odd way, it gave me closure in what my relationship with Earl was and used to be. I was able to pour into someone who was so different from me and yet the same in that we shared a brokenness and naive nature. Helping her was fufilling.

The signs of betrayal were all around me, but I was in too deep to notice. It started with her comparing her and Earl's relationship with how my relationship with him was. I found this to be strange and thought, *"Well, she's young."* The biggest moment of betrayal came well after the divorce and Earl's death. This young lady allowed jealousy and envy to come between us, and overnight she began to come for everything I had.

With no hesitation or remorse, this was a different kind of evil. She came for the ownership of some things, disregarding conversations Earl and I had when we divorced concerning how we would separate our possessions. It was such an absolute living nightmare that I kept pinching myself hoping to wake up. I even forgave her considering Earl had died and I knew she was wounded. I let her back in and then, I was hit with betrayal again. She took my kindness for granted. When I would take her to church, she would praise God next to me. I taught her how the business worked and yet, when the opportunity came, she fired up lawyers launching lawsuits against me and whatever else she could muster up.

That was the biggest betrayal that I've ever had, and it occurred when I was in my 50s. It was a blessing in disguise, however, because it changed me in a good way. I knew who God was and how the enemy worked. I was able to flip my perspective of everything. There's dark and light in this world, and the dark will really try to overtake you and have you living in a dark bubble if you allow it to keep you. Somehow, no matter how much the spirit of betrayal just wanted to sit on me, I've always managed to stay in the light. It may be dim and other times it may be bright. As long as it never goes out, I can say I kicked the spirit of betrayal into the Hudson River and watched it make its way downstream into the Atlantic.

I kicked it out of my childhood home even when it tried to creep back in when my mother showed up back into my life five years after she left. She knocked on the door of our home with a baby in her arms that was not my father's. Seeing him devastated that his own wife slept with another man was a tough watch. What truly made this sting was that my mother had slept with my grandfather—my dad's father—and had the audacity to pop up after her disappearing act with the product of her betrayal. A baby boy. My half-brother. I love him dearly, but the betrayal even affected him later on in his life.

We all experience betrayal at some point in our life. Think about what Judas did to Jesus. I look at that story and see the importance of Judas betraying Christ because that ultimately led Jesus to the cross where He died for all of our sins. As I continue to let my light shine and keep out that spirit I once knew like a best friend, I encourage others to do the same. Let your light source be an endless burning ember that nothing—and I mean *nothing*—will extinguish.

THE LESSON

SOME KEY TAKEAWAYS from my dealing with the spirit of betrayal on many occasions are as follows.

When people are broken, you have to pray for them.

I've met a lot of broken people in my life. There are the people who acknowledge their brokenness and are dealing with it on a deeper level. I've become friends with the majority of these people. Then there are these stray cats, people with a loud spirit whining and crying out in need of being heard. I see their brokenness. I see their shakiness. I see that old broken me, and I have a heart for these people. We must pray for them. We must pray *with* these people. I think back to my lowest point, and the power of prayer did numbers on my situation.

On that same note, I realize not every broken person is my responsibility. At one point, I felt as if they were because I was saving myself every time I came across a broken person. It really wasn't about them but me. I have to be very careful when I come across broken people because they do broken things. Despite all they do, a little prayer never hurt anybody.

Spell it out with me: "B-O-U-N-D-A-R-I-E-S."

This is something my parents taught me early on, something that really slipped to the back of my mind until this last betrayal. You have to protect your peace. You have to protect your mind, and you have to protect your light. You can't do any of this with a permeable boundary. Make it solid as a rock!

Know the signs, but don't live in fear of them.

At some point, I had to learn that not everybody is my mother, father, ex-husband, or even family members who betrayed me. You can sense it coming. I believe I am blessed with the spirit of discernment, so I most definitely could smell it when it was near. Asking for mental clarity, a sound mind, and the discernment to see signs of wicked betrayal can help prevent falling into its trap. The thing is though, you can't live in fear or anticipation of it. If you do, then what is the point of God? Can we not lean on Him? Can we not trust Him with all things and for Him to remove the works of the devil from our lives?

*Kiss bitterness, vengeance, and anger goodbye so you can stay in
the embrace of Jesus.*

Many people are angry or bitter and want revenge. They think, *"Well, this person hurt me. I'm going to hurt them."* In all of this, those were my initial feelings, but I had to really sit with myself and say, *"Tashera, that's not who you are."* Instead, know and follow the scripture.

> *Dearly beloved, avenge not yourselves,*
> *but rather give place unto wrath: for it is written,*
> *Vengeance is mine;*
> *I will repay, saith the Lord.*
> *(Romans 12:19)*

The Lord said what He said! I'm a true believer in karma. I don't believe that when you do me wrong, I need to reciprocate and do you wrong. I give it all to God. Fall into His sweet embrace and eventually the vengeance, the anger, and the bitterness will put a sour taste in your mouth.

THE OUTRO

IF I HAVEN'T made it clear, God is the source of my light. Yes, the enemy tried to take out that light by sending the spirit of betrayal, but did he win? He most certainly did not. My ex-husband was drawn to my light, but did I let him suck all of it out of me because he wanted it himself? No. My point is this: Jesus didn't walk around with His head down after Judas gave Him up. Yes, He saw it coming, but He continued to walk in His purpose and plan that He was to execute.

We can't let the enemy and his works keep us from living the life God has called us to live. There's too much work to be done and too much life to live to be stuck on a betrayal that happened five years ago or even last week.

THE AFFIRMATION

I am grounded in the unwavering
love of Jesus,
and no spirit of betrayal will dim the
light within me.

chapter ii

FLESH

There were times that if I had been in
my spirit and not in my flesh,
I would have seen a lot of people for
who they were.

Tashera Simmons

THE INTRO

WHEN SOMEONE pinches the fatty parts of their stomach or the fleshy parts of an inner thigh, they feel it. It's temporary pain. Eventually, he or she will no longer feel the pinch but rather a numbness. With that in mind, think of how the devil can get us so caught up in our flesh that we don't even feel what we're supposed to as we become numb to spiritual intervention or simple core values such as forgiveness and love.

Our flesh, our bodies, are organically unique. When we totally operate in the physical and focus on the bodily vessel that transports us from place to place, we miss out on so much. We don't thrive or move in higher places that God has called us to. Dying to self is when you kill your flesh and allow the spirit man to come alive. When your spirit really thrives, the fire and power take over. When you die to yourself, you feed your spirit because we are flesh and we are spirit. A lot of people I've come across unfortunately allow their spirit to lie dormant most of their life. If you feel as if your spirit has been dormant, I'm here to tell you how to get it to wake the hell up! But first, you have to slay all fleshly desires and temptations.

THE STORY

ONE EVENING, I found my mind falling deep into something rather peculiar and almost indescribable. I experienced the kind of moment that will get you sweating on a cozy night after the most perfect bottle of wine.

A light smoke filled the air as I navigated the space of dark archways and hallways of a place that I didn't quite recognize or know where I was. That was the allure of a place like that, a place to get lost. Men and women dressed elegantly in beautiful, ornate, masquerade-style masks were unknown to each other. They moved to each room to see what was happening. I adjusted my mask and smoothed out my dress as I nervously followed along so as not to be out of place. I heard something coming from the room everyone was heading to, sounds of pleasure. Part of me wanted to go see too.

"Oh, absolutely not!" I thought to myself as I came to a halt.

I let the others pass me and immediately took off in the other direction. I walked and walked until I made it somewhere quiet without people to catch my breath. I was alone, or so I thought. A man was leaning against a wall. Fine. Dark. Pretty teeth. His cologne was so strong. Dang. He came close to me, and I didn't back away. Before I knew it, we kissed. His hands traveled to where they weren't supposed to. Boom! We're in a different space. Darker. Hidden. Another man who was masked came behind me, and I was between both of them. I slowly took his mask off to see his face. It was a face that was not familiar.

"Tashera. Tashera, did you hear me?"

I snapped out of one of my deepest darkest fantasies just to realize my husband standing in front of me, keys in hand.

"I'll be back. I'm going to the studio," he said.

"Okay boo-boo, be careful."

I fixed my hair a bit and as the door shut behind him. I exhaled, hoping he didn't notice how far gone I was in my head. I checked the clock. A little past midnight. I had no idea he was going to another woman's house to do some of the same dark shit I fantasized about.

Let's be very clear readers. I'm sure we all fantasize some very dark shit while married! To me, that's the beauty of fantasizing. It's not real. Even though it had my flesh very riled up in real life, I don't think it was something I could have pulled off. I'm a one-woman man, always have been.

These fantasies became closer and closer together as the days went on, and I knew something was off. I was so wrapped up in my flesh that my spiritual ears were deaf and my spiritual eyes blinded. I continued to fall deeper and deeper into a pleasure-seeking haze. I loved sex so much, and that was easy to say with Earl around. He was all I had ever known for more than 30 years. My mind couldn't help but imagine beyond just him sometimes. I guess I never really had that exploration or sexual liberation that many people experience in their 20s and 30s. It got so dark that I started fantasizing about being with two men! The thought of that really excited me!

The spirit of conviction seeped in one day when a friend—a prayer warrior—gave me a call. I knew this was nothing but the Lord.

"God has a purpose for you, Tashera. He has a plan for you bigger than you know," she said as she ministered to me.

I responded, "I know, but I feel as if I have this sex demon inside of me. I have never felt so ashamed. The things I think about just ain't ordinary. I shouldn't be thinking about some of the stuff I do."

She prayed over me that night, and I felt as though that was my first moment when I realized that I needed my flesh to die right before me. It had to go. I was in a place that I liked far too much, and it would ultimately be my demise if I was not careful.

I found dating after Earl and I ended things to be particularly exciting. I looked forward to having sex almost too much. I thought back to the woman who prayed over me and decided, "No, I'm not going to give in to this desire."

I've come across people who struggle with lust and all things of the flesh who ask me, "Why can't we just live through life peacefully?" Guess what? We can if we die to our flesh. The flesh stinks. It's a foul stench saturated with toxicity. It just picks up everything like a sewer system. Dark. Dirty. A waste dump. It takes on anything—the wrong lovers, the wrong substances, or the wrong feelings toward someone.

Everything about emotions is the flesh. What do we feel? Our mind tells us, "I think he really likes me. He did this and he did that..." Meanwhile, he could be in a whole other relationship. Because you like the way he made you feel, you are ready to sacrifice whatever it takes and maybe even create a whole generational curse on yourself and your family due to feeling good at the moment. That is flesh.

If you are totally in your spirit, you will automatically know if someone is not for you. The Holy Spirit gives you revelation, but are you too caught up in your flesh to even hear Him? I know there were many times when I was. In the situation with Earl's girlfriend who I took in, the Holy Spirit tried to show me the situation was a love-hate relationship. She loved me because of the person I was being to her but hated everything about me because she couldn't be me. She did not have the spiritual strength, charisma, personality, love, notoriety, and the light that shined in me.

When you have the Holy Spirit in you, you have so much love for people. They could fuck you over so many times and you would still have that love for them. I've learned that with my ex-husband. No matter how many times he gave into his own flesh and slept with other women, I loved him. There was this constant battle between flesh and spirit within me. It wasn't until I decided that enough was enough that I allowed the spirit to win.

I remember being so in my flesh that I invited in depression and anxiety. Earl and I were having dinner with some friends one night when I just felt this sudden wave of anxiety. My breathing got heavier, and I felt every time someone laughed it was at me. I'm not sure if it was my guilt and shame over some of the thoughts I had been dealing with internally or if it was a spirit altogether, but what I do know is that I never experienced such anxiety when I was tapped into the spirit. I excused myself from the dinner table and ran upstairs to the bathroom. My heart rate quickened as I looked at myself in the mirror.

"Who even am I?" I asked myself.

Who I was before God was heavily involved in my life was different, and I thank Him for delivering me from some of the dark thoughts I used to have that would consume me. I threw cold water on my face and immediately there was this sizzle, a steam rising from my body as I cooled down from the blazing heat the spirit of anxiety had over me. I returned back to the dinner table feeling a bit of release, but the uneasiness was still there. I hated feeling that way, and I knew I couldn't continue to live like that.

In the industry Earl was in, it was not uncommon to succumb to the will of the flesh. He was bringing bad energy into our home. It stayed with me day and night. It felt heavy and held me in chains, crushing my spirit. It was almost as if I was a slave to my own body and mind. The enemy was busy, but he wasn't busy long enough to have taken me to a point of no return. We all have a chance at redemption and deliverance.

I had to do some deep work to get that sex demon off of me and to allow the spirit within to take over. Fasting in particular was a game changer for me. I remember starting off small after my marriage ended. I'd take away cheese. Then I'd try taking away all the dairy. Eventually I eliminated all meat, and that's why I am vegan today. My body began to repair itself from all the hurt and the trauma. I was being made whole again with every fast and every prayer. I even removed food entirely and only drank water and orange juice for 30 days. I fasted for 10 years total in order to heal from my last relationship. I went without TV, which is a whole other element that can open up doors and suggestions of the enemy. It seems so harmless, but you can lose your entire day sitting there watching and not dealing with your reality or things that you have to do. That was a big thing that I had to die to.

Ultimately, part of dying to self starts with killing the flesh. If you can shed the flesh like a snake sheds skin, you can truly find freedom and so much joy while walking in the spirit. It took me years to do this but when I finally did, I knew I was no longer a slave to something physical. Instead, I was a servant to someone who transcended beyond all of that. I was a daughter of Christ Jesus, and He had plans for me.

THE LESSON

BEING IN THE FLESH is easy. Fornicating is as easy as drinking water. It just happens, if we allow it. Being caught up in our emotions is inherently facile. All of it is not of God. Some key revelations that God showed me in order to allow my flesh to die are as follows.

Aim for 100% spirit 0% flesh,
but 90% spirit and 10% flesh is fine, too.

This principle recognizes that we are human, and we all fall short. Can we be 100% controlled by our inner-spirit rather than carnal desires of the flesh? Yes. When you embrace the anointing God has on your life and choose to say no to what feels good in the moment, you have access to this perfect ratio. Only one person was perfect, however, and it was neither you nor me. That's why I feel that even someone operating with 90% spirit and 10% flesh will conquer and walk into every single dream that they want for themselves. They will literally stumble upon what God has in store for them. How do I know that? Because I've done it. After my dad died, I wasn't at 100%. If anything, it was closer to 1% spirit and 99% flesh because I was in a dark place, depressed and confused. God always led me right back to the path I needed to be on nonetheless. Stay in the right spirit-to-flesh ratio and see what good things come about in your life.

Feed and allow the spirit man to thrive
and totally take control of your life

Who is the spirit man? He is the Holy Spirit. That sense of right and wrong within you is God Himself giving you discernment in your daily walk. Without Him, there is no moral compass. Anything goes. You may find yourself in a place of corruption and a state of wickedness without the spirit man guiding you in this frenzied world.

Feeding the spirit man can be done by reading the word, the bread of life. Staying knowledgeable in the spirit is key. How can you fight the enemy if you do not know the very word that makes him quiver and sweat? Feeding the spirit man will make it much easier to submit and allow God to take control of the reins. His will is perfect. When we operate outside of our flesh and let His Holy Spirit in, we win. That's it. We will win!

Fasting is how God's voice becomes loud.
Do your best to obey Him.

There were times when if I had been in my spirit and not in my flesh, I would have seen people for who they were. But I chose not to listen to God when He showed me red flags to warn me away from certain people. When I fasted, however, God's voice was undeniable.

It's like when you're at the grocery store and you see someone you don't want to talk to, so you go down a different aisle. Eventually, you end up nearly crashing shopping carts at the check-out line and are forced to talk. God is the same way. No matter how much you try to evade Him, He will find His way to you, and you better talk to Him. He has plenty to say, we just have to clear the noise and listen.

I know fasting can be difficult, but hear me out. Baby steps. Try it for 24 hours. Then a week. Once you see how you were able to overcome any urges, aim for 30 days. I started off small. Somehow, by God's grace, I was able to get to a place where I could fast from having sex for 10 years. I'm 10 years in. Pray for my strength! Be encouraged! Fasting changes things just like prayer does.

Remember that you may be in this world but you are not of it.

Always remember your Creator, who is not of this world. He walked on it in the form of a man. He was presented with the same temptations all around Him, but He did not fall victim to them. He cried out to His Father in times of trouble. You too can do the same. You too are not of this world. You may be here physically, but spiritually you can be in high places.

What can we learn from Jesus' story? He was never invested in satisfying His flesh because He knew His flesh would be stabbed and hung on a cross. He lived in His spirit. He understood that the flesh was so temporary. The more I got into the story of Jesus Christ and just seeing how He moved, I thought, *"God, I want to be more like your son."* We know the consequences of being in the flesh.

For the wages of sin is death; but the gift of God is eternal life through Jesus Christ our Lord. (Romans 6:23)

Jesus already paid the price for our sin. Stay in the spirit. Stay strong, and stay in the know. You may not be able to hang out with those girls who invite you over to drink wine and watch *Scandal* for the umpteenth time since it was put on Netflix. You may have to skip out on those festivities you've been partaking in since high school. You have to want to die to yourself bad enough that you are willing to lay your flesh down first. It isn't easy but oh man, it's rewarding.

THE OUTRO

PLEASE BE ADVISED that I am not judging anyone for fornicating or operating out of their flesh. People have a right to live however they please. Not everyone has a relationship with God, and many people don't even understand the purpose of drawing close to Him. All I can do is share what that relationship has done for me. As you will see, it strengthened me to go through spiritual warfare, endure a marriage filled with infidelity, and survive a toxic household in my adolescence.

Find God in the little things. Find God amongst friends and family. Most importantly, find God within. Although our bodies can be bruised, beat up, and bloody, our spirits are structurally sound and sturdy when we walk with God. Continue to let your flesh die so you can truly walk in spirit and in truth. Dying to flesh is the key to living in your true freedom that God has for you. If you really dig into his word, chains will be set free, and you will find liberty.

THE AFFIRMATION

I am free from earthly things
and will continue to seek things
of God and not of this world,
of his Spirit and not of my own flesh.

chapter iii

FAMILY

So many broken children grow to be broken adults, creating centuries of generational curses.

Tashera Simmons

THE INTRO

FAMILY IS THE CORE of who we are as humans, our very foundation. Unfortunately, not everyone's upbringing is positive, meaning countless children do not have the start they need in life to succeed. Even though I got to experience a glimpse of what healthy family life should look like in the first 14 years of my life, things took a turn. It could have shattered me into pieces but I learned early on, we have choices in life. It is like a game of checkers. Your next move is determined by whether you play conservatively or aggressively.

I never thought that my mother would turn her back on her family and leave us to fend for ourselves. How could you just leave your loved ones like that? That was her checker jumping over another one on the board. You can choose the values your family stands on, but you can't always choose what the enemy sends your way to split your family into many pieces that were destined to be whole.

THE STORY

GROWING UP IN YONKERS, I lived in a four-story building. People on my street of Linden and Park Hill Avenue and some of the surrounding blocks formed a true village. They say it takes a village, and I learned to appreciate this as I got older. I remember engaging in activities that I knew good and well I was not supposed to be doing. Ms. Shirley inevitably had to go and tell my mother. She was a short Italian woman who lived across the street. She had a mean disposition. Her clothes indicated that she spent a lot of time in the kitchen. To me at that time, she smelled like baked bread. I'm assuming she spent a lot of time baking.

My siblings and I would rush to go play with our friends after school. I'm talking about hopscotch and Ringolevio. It's a game with two teams, one of "hunters" and one of "prey." Both were so much fun and filled us with laughter. I really do remember being a joyous little girl despite the growing responsibility as my mother kept having my father's babies. As a 11-year-old girl, that's how it felt.

Right before I turned 11 years old, we were out on the block playing with a few kids. I was skipping through the squares during a quick round of hopscotch when I heard somebody from far away yell, "Oh, shit!"

There he was, my little brother John beating the crap out of some other dude. All the other kids rushed over to watch the fight of the season. Straight Ali vs. Frazier 1971 style upfront, live and center. Instead of screaming fans in an arena, we had girls with beads in their hair, hands covered in sidewalk chalk, and little boys with ashy knees with the grit of a weathered sugar Maple tree. I took one look at my friends around me and knew this was not going to end well. It was almost as if I was looking at them for the last time as the fight happened in slow motion. After this brief moment, I realized I had to do one thing: Protect my little brother. But then, he picked up a decent-sized rock and began busting the boy in the head.

"Stop it! Get off of him!" I yelled, but my voice was muffled behind all the noise.

Some other neighborhood kids broke up the fight. Around that time, there were a lot of children from different areas who played with us. Moments later at the house, I was doing what I could to take care of him before our parents got home from selling their incense. It was a ticking clock. I just knew we'd have hell to pay. Sure enough, that was the last time my siblings and I got to go out of the house. We kissed any social life outside of school goodbye that day.

My parents clamped down so much that I literally felt like my inner-child could not breathe from chewing on the bit so hard as the reins pulled in tighter and tighter. It would take years and my mother leaving in order for me to shake off the bridle of a strict household but at that moment, all I wanted to do was run free. I could tell my siblings wanted to as well.

We made the most of our time together in the house, my siblings and me. There were four channels on the only TV in the house—channels two, four, seven, and 11. I would switch through them one by one as we waited for our parents to come back from their hustle. We'd have to get creative when nothing but outside was on our minds. We dreamt of the twang of the grass we'd get a whiff of when we ran through it and the stinging feeling we'd get in our chest as we ran faster away from friends chasing us in the chilly, late-afternoon. Since we no longer had that, we created our own fun indoors the best way we knew how.

I feel as though my siblings and I missed out on some valuable lessons because we were cooped up inside out of harm's way. There were a few things I had to learn by watching other families, just simple observations I'd pick up, especially regarding the structure of a family. One thing that my family struggled with a lot as I was growing up was communication. Have you ever felt like no matter what you do or say, someone is looking straight through you or above you like you're not even there? Well, that's how I felt. I had no say in anything. I was expected to shut-up and listen, do whatever I was told, and keep it pushing.

Not once was I asked how I felt about something. Not once was I asked if I would be okay if *"XYZ"* was done instead of *"ABC."* No one talked about respecting one another or each other's feelings. It's as if we didn't have a right to have feelings. If you follow what I'm putting down here, you know that voiceless children often do the loudest things to be seen and heard once they get older. Overlooked children face fear of abandonment and rejection as adults as well.

When I was 13, I really noticed the level of respect my father had for me being his first girl and all. He taught me to wait to have sex. He'd say things such as, "Save your cookies for someone who's worthy, who shows you respect, and for someone who loves you."

"Yes sir," I replied.

"You a queen, and don't you ever forget that. You need to love yourself too."

I loved hanging out with him in those early years. By 14 after my mother left, he sort of eased up on the restrictions. As much as I hated that time in my life, I was actually able to get back to the outside world with friends. I got a job at Burger King and was able to make a contribution to the family. I even later went on to live with my godmother, a good woman who instilled in me a lot of pertinent qualities that intertwined with the many things that made me who I am today.

Family dynamics are not the same in every household but in her home, she made sure I knew what boundaries were. When my parents were together, I saw the need for boundaries and structure in that household but with my godmother, the vibe was completely different. Growing up under my parents' household, it was as if we were all put in the same pot but we weren't separated, and that's why I felt overlooked. At the end of day, I feel my parents did the best that they could. My godmother, however, still was like a mother figure and put me in my place at times. She would not only tell me to refrain from doing something but would tell me why, which is very important with children. With her, I learned what makes a home.

People really overlook children because of how young they are, but they are sponges and they're soaking in everything. Every move that you make is really vital because they're watching. We are their role models. Looking back, I thank God I did not follow in my parents' footsteps with my four children. I often would ask them things such as: "How do we feel? What are you going through? What challenges are you facing in life? Are you dating? Do you like someone?" I would literally take time at least once every other week to get an update on how everyone felt and how we were creating boundaries in our lives for people who steal our energy, happiness, and peace.

To this day, my kids demonstrate some of the values I ingrained in them from an early age. They are attentive, they listen, they pay attention to things and how people feel. Sometimes they do so to a fault because people are so broken and never had someone to even listen to them, so it can become a little awkward. When one of my sons talks to you, he looks you in your eyes. He told me of one instance he had with a person he was conversing with that went a little something like this:

"Why are you looking at me like that?"

My son responded, "Because I'm listening."

"Wow. I never had anyone listen to me without looking around to other places. They're typically not listening, for real."

I imagine my son shrugging it off as if it was nothing with all his humbleness, but he told me this was a recurring thing with his good friends. They truly appreciated his attentiveness.

I refused to allow my children to fall into demonic-like depression, poor health, and self-hate. I refused. We absolutely stayed prayed up. My father watched me work so hard on my children and he joined in, despite all his bad habits. He followed my lead and used to tell me all the time how proud he was of me in the way I handled them. I used to get annoyed when he said that because maybe I did have a little resentment toward him. It wasn't the type of resentment that festers and bubbles to a surface but more like a "Let me show you how it should have been done" attitude. I am so blessed to have four beautiful children who have now grown up.

My own siblings made it out alive as well. Two of them, my brothers, lost their minds. One of them returned to lucidity, but the other one has yet to fully recover after being in the streets so long. I often wonder how he would have ended up if our mother would have stayed or if our father didn't end up the way he did. Family, no matter where everyone ends up, will always be a thread in the fabric of our identity and our place in the world.

THE LESSON

THROUGHOUT MY YEARS on this earth, I've had childlike eyes and wonder regarding the structure of families and what makes them great as well as what causes them to crumble. Following are some takeaways.

Communication is not just key, it's the key,
the keyhole, and the door.

Don't treat people as if they don't have a mind and a voice. This is the old school way of doing things. We live in a time where now more than ever people are expressing their ideas, thoughts, and creativity as they speak out against injustices. Why not let communication be number one in your home and in your family? Yes, difficult conversations are uncomfortable, but that doesn't mean you just don't have them.

My dad did it all the way till he passed. I felt like he got better with it toward the end of his life, but I used to always tell him about himself. It was like beating him with a bat when it came to communication and in the end, he didn't even communicate that he was sick. This man was dying. I had never seen anything like it before. He knew he was dying, yet he did not say anything and did not communicate it. He had so many times to talk to me about it but was stuck in his ways. He didn't even communicate certain things with us growing up. It's absolutely unacceptable. God rest his soul.

Generational curses must go at all cost. It starts with you.

Do you ever catch yourself turning into your mother or father, doing to your kids some of the same things that they did to you? So many broken children grow to be broken adults, creating centuries of generational curses. When will the cyclical patterns of behavior end? Generational curses persist because people follow the same broken lessons, habits, and ways from their upbringing. For me, all it took was another idea, another way out, another person who just happened to be my godmother. We have to come against some of these curses that trickle down the family tree. It's not what God wants for his children.

How do we break the cycle? One, recognize it exists. Two, determine why it exists. Three, introduce new thoughts, ideas, and people who identify the problem and communicate better than you do. If your daddy was a rolling stone and you find yourself doing the same thing, pause, think, and surround yourself with somebody who is stable and steady. If your mother was an alcoholic, pause, think, and surround yourself with people who have been sober for 10 years and counting. That stuff that is passed down is no joke!

Create a space for respect and
watch peace invite itself in your home.

I realized how important boundaries were, and I've somehow taught my children without even realizing what I was doing. I emphasized boundaries, such as to respect one another. If little Bobby wants some alone time in his room with his favorite toy, little Sarah has to learn to respect him enough not to burst through the dang door and rip it out of his hands to play with it herself! Respect is simple to me, but it can become complicated at times. Yes, it's typically earned. But true love in a family means giving it no matter how that other person makes you feel. When your husband is cussing at you because he is heated and overworked, is it on you to disrespect him the best way you know how? A house without respect is a space where chaos can reign. That's what the devil wants, and we can't have that now can we?

THE OUTRO

NO MATTER WHAT your family dynamics may be, know that it's the core of who you are. It's your beginning and your end. We are born into a family and a lot of us leave a family behind after we exit this world. There's no escaping it. Even if you are estranged, somebody in your bloodline exists somewhere. Keeping God at the center of everything will give a home peace that passes all understanding. Remember God's word.

> *Train up a child in the way he should go:*
> *and when he is old,*
> *he will not depart from it.*
> *(Proverbs 22:6)*

It starts with you. You can break any generational curse that hovers over you. Make the decision. Make it fast because you may have little ones watching, and not just the ones of your own blood. Sometimes, there's a little boy or girl who might see in you the ideal family they one day want to achieve. I know this because that little girl was me.

THE AFFIRMATION

There is mutual respect, love, and connection between my family members and myself, and I will not let anything get in between that.

chapter iv

MARRIAGE

We knew what each other was
thinking just by looking at each other.
We had our own language by
our eyes.

Tashera Simmons

THE INTRO

CALL ME A LOVER GIRL or whatever you want to, but I love love. Love is everything. It's kind. It's patient. God is love. It is through a covenant between two people who truly love each other in sickness and health, richness or poverty, death or life where love manifests in beautiful ways like I've never seen before. I love marriage to the point where I'd consider getting married again one day. I believe in it as an institution and everything it stands for.

What I don't believe in is the perversion of love, the corruption of it or the outright disrespect of it. Marriage is not something to be played with. It's not something you just wake up and decide to do. If you think about everything involved in a marriage—the assets, the children, the extended families—you start to wonder if it is even worth it. As we discover the ins and outs of marriage, understand that part of dying to self is also understanding that we can learn a lot from such a covenant between two people and God. Through that we can also learn how love can transform any grudge, dissolve any hatred, and dismantle any nefarious spirit that latches onto any holy thing it can find.

THE STORY

I CAME HOME from the grocery store one beautiful August afternoon with more groceries to carry than my hands could manage. The kids weren't home just yet. Earl had them for a brief moment while I had work to get done. Earl was good with helping me out when our nanny was off. I set the groceries on the island and made my way back to the car to get the last of them.

The mailwoman pulled up to the house, and I figured I'd just meet her and get the mail directly from her. Part of me wondered why the mail was running so early, but I pushed the thought to the back of my mind.

"Thank you. You have yourself a nice day," I said while taking the mail from her.

I turned my back, mail and grocery bag in hand.

"Wait. This is also for you," she said.

I turned around to a big manilla envelope, you know the kind. I looked at the mailwoman briefly, just enough to catch a sense of pity in her eyes.

When I went inside the house, I didn't even think much of what was in the envelope. I was in a rush to get the groceries put up so I could have a moment to myself before the kids came. As I placed the last thing of orange juice in the refrigerator, I looked over to the island where the thick envelope was just sitting there.

I turned it over to see the return address was for some surrogate court type of place where people sue for child support and all that. Basically, some woman was claiming Earl was her child's father. The pain was so severe that I felt it physically. In my chest. In my stomach. I think something happens in our minds when we encounter emotional pain. I've read where our bodies can't differentiate between what hurts physically and mentally. This most definitely was an overwhelming feeling. I wasn't even initially comprehending what I was reading because the pain came so severe. It was almost as if I didn't even want to believe what I was reading.

There was a disconnect, almost a "This does not compute" error code you'd see on an old dusty computer. I couldn't even possibly begin to contemplate my marriage with Earl. I just couldn't believe he would do such a thing. There was no way. Not my Husband.

We started dating when I was 17 years old. He was the same age as me and had this walk about him. The way he talked too, it was obvious he just knew he was the shit. Crazy enough though, he's the one that brought me to Christ. He loved his God, and I wanted to love that same God. I wanted something to believe in and something to stand for.

That first week he met me he said, "I'm going to get married to you."

I laughed at him because he was just bluffing, surely.

"I'm serious. I'm gonna marry you girl."

Little did I know, we'd be down to the altar years later. At the time, I felt his deep love. That's when I let him in. He was always traveling. I was there most of the time, but his career was taking off right before my eyes. It was the fastest thing. I've never seen nothing like that before. It was like he went from nobody to somebody overnight. We couldn't even go into stores or shopping centers without folks running us out. We had to run back to our car. His stardom started kicking in, and I was along for the ride of a lifetime.

When we first started dating, he came from a house with his mom who had four kids—three girls and one boy. There were four baby fathers. Even though my mom left, we all shared the same dad, so that was just a level of parenting that I never really experienced. His type of home was not completely uncommon, but you could always spot it out when you saw it. Other children noticed it growing up. I'd often get asked if me and my siblings had the same dad.

Earl looked at me weeks after we had started dating and told me, "When I have children, I want to have them by one woman because I know what it feels like to be shuffled around or neglected or not even have a father at all."

I could tell this was coming from his soul when he said this, so I believed every word that came out of his mouth. We were together 10 years before we married. The connection that we had was just so insane. It was almost as if we could finish each other's sentences. We knew what each other was thinking with just a glance. We had our own language using our eyes. We were so close and being married just took it to another level. There were no signs, no red flags. Anyone who knew me and him knew he was very affectionate and very outspoken about me. Everybody knew because it was on social media. Oftentimes, he'd say affirmations such as, "This is my wife. Be careful. Watch out, move."

When we went places, he would be really aggressive about letting people know who I was and demanding they respect me. So when I received those papers in that manilla envelope years later, I was devastated and baffled.

It was truly unbelievable. I didn't want to accept that somebody I was so close with and shared such deep love with would hurt me like that to the point where he would not even protect himself. I never thought about him sleeping with other people, but I never put it past him. This may sound crazy, but I always knew where his heart was.

I had brothers, and I had a lot of solid relationships with men who were good friends. They used to talk about the difference between cheating and loving someone, and it used to all sound insane to me. Then I started to realize that not all men look at relationships the same way. If they sleep with someone, it doesn't equate to love. They just wanted to be with a woman. So maybe in the back of my mind, I had that understanding, but it wasn't something I dwelled on. To see there was somebody saying that they had a child by him was beyond cheating.

I know that children are blessings from God, but what kind of woman would want to intentionally break a family apart? You had to be under a rock not to know that DMX was married. He talked about it in every interview on the radio. I was in two of his videos. There's no way she didn't know. I understand some women say as a defense, "Well he told me this" or "He didn't have a ring on." You mean to tell me if a man told you the sky was purple, you'd believe it without going to look and see yourself? I try to be understanding, I really do, but this was beyond my comprehension.

When Earl came home with the kids, I played it cool for as long as I could. I had to call on Jesus to keep me from literally exploding. Later that day, I confronted him about it. At first he cried rape, which is something you are never supposed to do, especially for the sake of those who have experienced such trauma. It makes it harder for people and police to believe accusers when such a crime does happen. That was a cowardly move on his part, but on with the next excuse. He claimed he didn't remember. He was drunk. My pain only increased when the woman went public and talked about having a baby in her effort to extort money. He went public too, speaking in interviews and being quoted in magazines asserting that he was drunk.

"How did you not know this? You think these women really want you? They want your money. You have a wife and a family at home. You have a real foundation at home that has no cracks, and I'm riding and dying for you. Why would you even be this sloppy?" I had to say it to him.

The conversation went on and on. The more circles we talked in, the more overwhelmed I felt but eventually, I prayed on it. Given our long history and the importance of keeping my family together, I chose to give him another chance and move on. Was it a mistake? Was I setting myself up for more heartbreak? I had three kids at the time, and there was no way I was letting some woman shatter our family.

There were others—women who treated me and my kids as if we were the problem, as if they were the wife and I was the baby mother with four kids. How backwards! How insulting to the institution of marriage. One thing about marriage is that it is not only a covenant with God and your spouse, but it is a legal agreement. When people are married, they are legally entitled to things. Earl and I shared a business, and he really taught me a different side of entertainment that I would've never gotten into had we not married. All our assets, everything we built together was in jeopardy due to these obsessive women he had fawning over him. These were women who went to church, played in God's face by performing rituals of praise and prayer just to not truly believe in God's design for marriage. God put adultery on the same level as murder for a reason. It's an absolute abomination. But one thing is for certain, I was not going to let his cheating steal my peace or my joy.

I realized that none of this was ever about me. His choices had nothing to do with not loving me. It was all about his quest to find love for himself that he never had with his own mother. It was bigger and deeper than me. We started so young that I wasn't the wise woman I am now.

THE LESSON

DESPITE EVERYTHING, marriage is a beautiful thing from God Himself. Following are a few take-aways from my experience.

Do the work, and do it together.

If I could turn back the clock and do things all over again, or if I ever get the chance to marry again, I'd have different conversations with my spouse-to-be. I'd find out about his goals and aspirations. Why does he even want to get married?

Marriage counseling with a pastor can be something to do together. We could make a day out of it and maybe go to dinner afterward. The point is, do the pre-work to really figure things out before committing to marriage. Get aligned spiritually beforehand. There's nothing worse than playing catch up just to realize y'all are not equally yoked.

Don't take marriage lightly or it will take you,
maybe even into the hole financially!

I'm not being pessimistic. Let's keep it real. Some divorces end in some deep doo-doo. One partner loses millions of dollars to a spouse or that favorite couch. You cannot take marriage lightly because there are laws set in place so that once you are married, ownership is split. It's a union. What was once yours becomes ours. What was once "I" and "me" very quickly becomes "we" with a simple "I do." Marriage is nothing to fool around with.

Enact God's original will for married couples
and watch your love be rewarded.

It was never in God's will for you to be unfaithful to your spouse, and it was never His will for your spouse to be unfaithful to you. You know I had some dark fantasies about men who were not my husband. I made the choice not to ever act on anything. You have to respect your partner enough and God's covenant made between the both of you before many witnesses every time you see that fine woman from the fifth floor in the elevator. You have to respect that same covenant when the guy at the gym flirts with you. Fight back what is so fleshly and tap into what is higher. When you made that covenant, you agreed to put your husband or wife above all else. Any time you realize you are not doing that, it is not living in God's will. Get back aligned and remember the love God has for you personally. You can then channel that love and spread it to your spouse, your kids, even the dog! Make it a contagious love, an unfailing love, and watch how God blesses you and your family.

THE OUTRO

I'LL SING IT till the cows come home. Actually no, I won't. City girl here, through and through. I love all the different kinds of love. Agape (Godly), Eros (Romantic), and Philia (Friendship). They exist for a reason, and God made us to share the love of Christ among all whether they deserve it or not.

Are you still redeemable after being unfaithful to your husband on several occasions? You most certainly are. Are you still accepted by the beloved after going to the strip club even though your wife has your location on her phone? Absolutely. No one is too far from grace. Keep love as an anchor in the sea despite torrential rain. Love yourself enough to know what you will stand for and what you want. Most importantly, remember to kill off that spirit of lust and infidelity to unleash that golden, warm center of who you truly are.

THE AFFIRMATION

I understand that marriage is a
sacred covenant.
I will not allow the distractions of the
enemy to take what God has blessed
me with beyond measure.

chapter v

SPIRITUAL WARFARE

When I started to be educated on how
the spiritual realm works,
I realized I was at war and it wasn't
about me anymore.

Tashera Simmons

THE INTRO

THE SPIRITUAL REALM is an unseen world that transcends beyond the physical realm we call earth. We all are made up of spirit, soul, and body so of course there are things that can disrupt each of these individual levels of our being. Spiritual warfare is the constant battle that's going on in the spiritual realm. I started opening up my eyes to it in 2006, which was actually when I and my ex-husband started having problems. I started to see the evil in people and the shifts that take place underneath the surface. These shifts occur almost like tectonic plates moving. Incognito and off the radar until, boom! An earthquake. Shifts that were unseen, hidden beneath result in something very real, shaking, and physical.

All I can tell you is that spiritual warfare is indeed a bloody battle. Nothing about it is pristine, clean, or simple. The question is, are you suited for battle? Are you prepared to fight? Not fighting with your hands or fighting with a tongue filled with quick words that cut like daggers. You have to be prepared to fight with your spiritual weapons that God has equipped you with because without them, you could very well be slayed beyond your spirit. There is room for spillage into our soul and even our body therefore, we have to know what war we are fighting and how to win it every day.

THE STORY

TEARS STREAMED DOWN my face as I settled on my closet floor. I'm not exactly sure when this was, but I know I was still with Earl and was crying over him. I began to question God. *"If you were real, you would show yourself to me,"* I said in my head. The tears just kept coming. That closet floor soaked up so many of those same tears over the years. That's what happens when you put up with the same things for so long. I kept my eyes closed in the dark. The clothes were stacked in a way that kept any light from coming in. The closet was enormous and sort of extended beyond a corner. Before I knew it, I felt this warmth. When I looked up, I saw a light green luminance coming from around the corner. I immediately thought one of my children opened up my closet door. I wiped my eyes so they wouldn't catch me in such an emotional state. Then I realized the closet door was still closed! The light began to move closer toward me, so I busted out of that closet so fast! *"What could that possibly be?"* I thought to myself. I had felt so warm around whatever it was. That's when I knew I was dealing with some sort of spirit. There were no eerie or uneasy feelings because this spirit was good. Considering everything I had said to God, maybe it was Him. This was not my only encounter with the supernatural spirit realm. In fact, the enemy had plans of attack.

That encounter forever did something to my spirit. It gave me a sense of comfort subconsciously. Moving forward through hurtful situations, I knew the spirit of God was always watching over me. As we all know, the devil is always busy and unfortunately the hurtful trials continue to come.

That was certainly true for me during the separation from Earl, which was very traumatic for my children. It led to a lot of trapped trauma and bombarded their mental growth. It was as if gradually the spirits of abandonment, depression, and suicide all came to knock on their doors. They did not knock politely. I did my absolute best to help my children fight those spirits whether they opened the door or not. I thought I could fill in for my kids as their dad stepped out on them and went on to be with other women, but I soon came to realize no mother can fill that void. The hole created by his absence, which I thought I had sutured up with all the love and support I could give, would soon be revealed to be a ruptured wound much deeper than ever imagined.

I was seeing a generational curse trickle down from my mother's side and my father's side as well. My mother was abandoned by her mother. My father was also abandoned by his mother. Then here we were with a father, Earl, basically walking out on his family. I wasn't as spiritually equipped as I should have been, so there was a war going on unbeknownst to me between myself and between my own children. In a sense, the devil had already won the moment that the void opened up in my kids' lives. The generational curse germinated and caused things to fester. This could eventually lead to the continued cycle with my children's children, and I could not let this stand. This spiritual battle was far from over.

It's about the children and generations to come, the future families. Their destiny starts with our actions. Which way are we going to go? Left or right? We better stay right because if we go left, we have no idea where that road may lead or what it's going to affect. I've spoken to many women and men who walked out and were not intentionally trying to hurt their children. They walked away and didn't follow through. It's not what you do, it's how you do it. If you have outgrown someone, you still have a responsibility to the souls that you created together with another person.

When I started to become educated on how the spiritual realm works, I began to realize that I was at war, and that the outcome wasn't about me anymore. It was about my four children! The generational curses stop with me! The only reason why a generational curse is able to plague an entire bloodline for centuries is because we are not equipped to engage in spiritual warfare. We lack the knowledge and power of the Holy Spirit. My four children will be fully equipped to fight the spirit of hurt, depression, suicide, etc. Watching their innocent and pure hearts be violated hurt the most. All they knew was that they saw two happy parents who lived in the home, disciplining and teaching them. Three out of those four dealt with deep depression. Two out of four dealt with the spirit of suicide. The devil seeks for the opportunity to send these spirits in to fill voids, open doors, and smother you with thoughts that are not of God. You have to sharpen your spiritual weapons.

From an early age, I impressed upon my kids' little minds that there were powers at bay. I wouldn't scare them by any means, but I was able to finesse it and say to them, "When we look at certain superhero movies, even ghost movies, this is the world that you guys are dealing with."

They would look at me so pure hearted and interested in what I was telling them. I was speaking truth. When I look back to that moment in the closet, the warmth I felt, that was real. On the other hand, the spirit of rejection that swept through my kids' rooms and stole their joy in the night was also very real. I could see it on them. They felt like their father didn't want them anymore.

When you have talents that can take you to where God is calling you to be, you don't even know who you are. You can't even move forward because when you do go for that interview or try to tap into your spiritual gifts and talents that God has instilled in you, you keep hearing you're not good enough. You're not going to be able to accomplish that. They're going to tell you "No" because the spirit of rejection has lived deep down in your soul for so many years. That spirit is rooted in having been rejected by your earthly father, the one who is supposed to teach you to keep going to know who you are, to love yourself regardless of what you do. This is what my kids would soon face from being abandoned at such an early age.

You have to learn to put on your spiritual coat and teach your children that the weapons of our warfare are not carnal. Real spirits surround us, flooding our minds everywhere we go. I'd tell them, "Mama can be with you every day of the week and every hour and minute but when you guys go off the college, when you start to date and have a new friend group, spirits will be lurking and looking for a way to get in to tear you down. That way you will spiral to a place that the enemy hopes you cannot get out of. I'm telling you now, the teaching starts here. You see what your mother has gone through. Learn from that."

I instilled in them and myself Ephesians 6:12 which states that *We wrestle not against flesh and blood* and to *put on the whole armor of God.* Let me emphasize the words "full armor." You don't just put on a helmet when you go to war, right? You put on the whole getup, and then you hop up on that black stallion and lead the charge of the army's vanguard. The helmet of salvation, breastplate of righteousness, sword of the spirit, belt of truth, shield of faith, and gospel of peace shoes need to be on tight and firm.

I also raised them to be prayer warriors. I have prayer warriors amongst me and I see it in my children. To this day, I often hear them praying. They tell me, "Mom this is a situation, and we have to pray about it!" And my response is always, "Yes! You're right because there is power in prayer. You realize that even though your girlfriend just out of nowhere said she needed to take a break, or you didn't get this job, or you can't find good friends in college, or whatever the case may be, taking it to the Lord in prayer is always the best way to go."

The spirit of loneliness, the spirit of betrayal, the Jezebel spirit of immorality, the spirit of fear—they all come from a lowly place we can't always see. Sometimes, like that moment God gifted me in the closet, your spiritual eyes may get a glimpse between realms and catch spirits of light that will guide you to a place where God has you covered. Just like I was able to see that spirit of light, I've come across spirits of evil and even demonic forces. You will find that the armor you put on when encountering spirits of depression and the like is the same armor needed when you encounter the darker forces from the bowels of hell.

THE LESSON

THERE ARE SO MANY nuggets to give you, but following are a few key takeaways.

My life changed when I began to put on the armor of God every day. The scales dropped off of my eyes, and I perceived life differently. God prepared me for the war I would have to soon face.

No matter how many storms come,
you need to know the word of God.

When you have a revelation of what God's word says about you, it changes who you are. You are no longer in the battle alone. I know I will not fall. Why? I have now built my life on a firm foundation. My assignment is to help build people connecting to me. Growing up, I heard the elders say, "Don't build on sand or sinking rock, but on a firm foundation." As an adult, I understand it now. When you are planted in the word of God, you can't be moved. You will hear lies, but you know the word of God is true.

The word says, if you believe in the Lord
and take Him up in your heart, He will be there.

I watched my children go through a lot of personal storms as they aged throughout the years. Without having the spirit of the Lord, you are an open door for so many other spirits to come in. I taught them to put on their armor as soon as they wake up daily and before their feet touch the ground. You have to be protected every day because the enemy will come for you any way he can. You have to protect your eye and ear gates. Remember the storms only come for a little while, and the rainbow God promised us will show up.

We have to be responsible for our actions
because what the future holds
as a result of someone else's choices is always bigger than us.

I thank God I took the route to be counseled by my pastor. You have to seek wise counsel. This offered me the ability to learn more about God and how the spiritual realm works. One thing that I've learned is that God doesn't consider one sin bigger than any other. It was never about me and my ex-husband. It was about the souls our marriage was supposed to affect. We loved to take in children and minister to them. God used His supernatural presence through us to help fight the spiritual warfare on earth. Without knowing it, your life speaks volumes. You could be the second mother or father to a lot of single-parent-home children.

I take my role of mentoring impressionable young minds very seriously. I always teach young people about the love of God and that His word never fails. It's not about what they see but always about what the word of God says. When children transition into different ages and hormones, they become easy targets of the enemy. They want to fit in. It's a lesson I know all too well from my own children. Be the one who changes the life of young ones. Teach them to fight.

When you start to feel depression, it's not of God.

Depression is a spirit and will take you into dark, deep places. Trust me. Using my armor I was able to get it off of me. The spirit of depression, death, and suicide tend to be in collaboration to keep you from purpose. Self-hate is right around the corner, waiting to pounce on you if depression doesn't get you. The issue you must understand is they are all not from God. This is why God constantly tries to teach us to know who we are. We are beings on earth rooted in Christ, and we know how to fight these spirits. Warfare is not our portion. Always remember we carry the fruits of the spirit.

But the fruit of the Spirit is love, joy, peace, longsuffering,
gentleness, goodness, faith, meekness, temperance:
against such there is no law.
(Galatians 5:22-23)

God so easily lets us know what it looks like to have His spirit. Fruit shows up in multiple ways. God gives us fruit and armor to win every spiritual war.

THE OUTRO

FOR THE LONGEST TIME, I thought I was conditioned to think everything happened in the physical world. This is what we do in our day-to-day lives. We fight sickness and disease and verbally fight with each other. What I soon found was that beneath the surface, there was a spiritual level to it all. Whether it is the spirit of perversion whispering in your ear or a jealous spirit meeting you in the mirror every morning, you may not be able to see them with those two balls in the sockets of your skull! If you continue to pray and ask for discernment, fast, and put on your full armor daily, you are counterattacking every single attempt of advancement by the enemy.

It's up to us to claim victory. The battle was already won when Jesus died on the cross for us. I may have thought the devil won against my family at several moments in my life, but look who is still standing. Look who is still fighting. Yes, the fight seems as if it will go on forever, but if we remember the main fight was already won, all these little battles feel minute. The enemy attempts to convince us they are more blown up than what they actually are. They are not the battles that define us. The war stories and scars will be deep in our history, but what the enemy can't steal from us is our battle cry. He can't steal our prayer language. He can't steal us from our own camp and keep us in his for all eternity when we've already chosen the winning side.

THE AFFIRMATION

I am dressed and fully equipped in
the armor of God.
The victory is mine today, tomorrow,
and forever with the strength and
guidance of my Lord Jesus Christ.

chapter vi

DEMONIC

I was fighting a demonic battle not only in my life but my children's lives.

Tashera Simmons

THE INTRO

HAVE YOU EVER found yourself observing something strange and unexplainable? Something that didn't sit well with you? Or have you ever had a feeling of heaviness that could not be medically explained? I'm here to tell you, the forces of evil never rest. I've encountered evil on many occasions and each time, I had to call on Jesus. There's no other name that can make the enemy wither away.

There were women who sent demonic forces after me and my children that entered and disrupted my home and disturbed me to my core. How can you sleep when these malicious acts are going on? The darkness that clouds the minds of humans who serve a master other than the Lord can tower over others and really test their sanity. This is a playing field where you will start to ask, "Is what I'm seeing actually real?" Stay locked in with God, and these demonic forces won't stand a chance. However, you can't always control what they do to your children, your marriage, or your own health. They move with intention and they want to succeed. You get to choose how you react to any situation. Trust and know God is in control.

THE STORY

IN THE MIDDLE of the night, I heard a scuffle in the closet. I was maybe 9 years old and shared a room with my brother. I looked over and saw him turn to his side. He was sound asleep. I envied him, as I hadn't been able to rest all night because of what I knew would be awaiting me in the closet. This wasn't some childhood monster. This was something much more vile and wicked. I almost didn't get up to go look, but I could not rest.

As I approached the closet, I felt a cold chill run up from my tail bone to the top of my spine. Quickly, I open up the closet door. There she was. The woman. I'd seen her many times before. She was swinging on the clothes hanging line, as if she were a piece of clothing bobbing, bouncing up and down. Her face was so evil, and she maintained eye contact with me as she swung up and down, back and forth. This woman was an evil spirit or maybe even a demon, but I didn't know it at the time. All I knew was that every time I saw her, I did not feel good in my spirit. She smiled at me as she saw how uncomfortable I looked when she stared at me. She jumped out of the closet! I took no time to run back to my bed and hide under the covers. My brother awoke immediately due to my swiftness and some odd sounds that probably escaped my mouth.

"You okay, Tashera?" he asked me.

"Yeah."

I could feel the beads of sweat sticking to my pajamas. My body trembled in fear. It was an uncontrollable trembling.

"I'm just scared," I said.

"Are you afraid of the woman in the closet?" he asked, joining me under the covers.

"Yes."

I couldn't say much more, but him joining me was a comfort, and I knew she wouldn't show herself with my brother there with me.

The woman in the closet wasn't the only spirit I saw as a child. Before my mom left, I would see them often. Sometimes I'd see people dressed in old-time clothing or big flannels. One time I was in my room, and it was pitch black. There was a little girl in there with me. She was close and even though it was dark, I could see her and nearly reach out to touch her. She didn't have the same energy as the evil woman so I guess she was a good spirit, maybe even a ghost.

Feeling the presence of spirits and seeing them was not my only spiritual gift. Sometimes I would have visions, including one with water by the washing machine. I thought, *"What is that?"* My eyes opened as if I was daydreaming, and then a premonition came. The next day, my father called out to me. He was in distress.

"What's up?" I came to him.

"The washing machine is flooding. It's overflowing!"

I said, "Disconnect it! Take the plug out."

The water kept flowing and flowing causing the levels to rise. He had been trying to figure out how to get it to stop. Because I saw this happening the day before, I was not too worried about the situation but rather mesmerized at how accurate it was. I didn't know if it was God starting to speak to me and tell me about a bunch of things that were going on or what.

As an adult I still found myself dealing with the supernatural, especially around my marriage. There seemed to be attack after attack. This was when I discovered the importance and power of prayer. I got married in my 20s and had no idea the enemy loves coming after the union of marriage. It's the perfect target. When Earl and I separated but were still married, my children and I were really going through it. I would pray to God asking for my husband's return to our home. My minister, Pastor Hazel, always told me that when you pray, it has to come from your heart and soul so that's what I did because I was so desperate. The separation was so devastating for me because it was a trigger to my past as far as a failed relationship, a failed marriage, or a failed family. I never wanted to repeat that. I worked so hard to make sure that I didn't make the same mistakes. I know what it felt like to live in a broken home, and I didn't want that for my children. So I thought, *"I gotta make this work,"* but my ex-husband was so out of order that I dealt with him in the spiritual realm.

First I just started praying, and then I started to learn how there was so much power in fasting. I started fasting for 30 days with just water and was around the clock with prayer. My kids were young. They were in school. I got up. I filled my whole mornings with the word channel because I was just doing research. I surrounded myself with spiritual people despite every other nosey person who wanted to know what was happening with my marriage. I really tried to keep people out of my business but Earl was a public figure and because of it, our lives were public.

One night as I was fasting, I was reading the Bible and fell asleep with it on my stomach. I heard a hissing sound like a snake. I'm a very light sleeper, so I heard it and immediately questioned it. Was there an actual snake in the room? I was half asleep and it sounded like it got closer and closer. Then, the hissing was in my face! I woke up. I told Pastor Hazel about it.

"There is someone trying to put witchcraft on you," she said calmly but sternly.

"What? Witchcraft? Is that even real?" I responded perplexed. I knew about spirits, but witchcraft felt like a whole new territory.

"It's very real."

Every night after that, I continued to wake up and feel the presence of someone in the room. Being a light sleeper, I could always tell when someone else was in the room. I'd wake up all the time when my kids tried to sneak into bed with me. I was waking up in the dark at 3:15 a.m. on the dot every night and no one was in the room, so of course I was concerned.

"That time of day is the hour of witches and demons," Pastor Hazel said to me over the phone.

I thought to myself, *"This is the type of stuff that only happens in movies!"*

"I want you to say, 'I rebuke you in the name of Jesus' the next time you wake up and feel that spirit in the room."

I thought about this for a while. Would it actually work? Would this agony and feeling of restlessness truly end? That next night, I felt someone enter the room.

"I don't know who or what you are, but I rebuke you in the name of Jesus! Leave right now," I called out into the night.

There was a calmness in the room, and I was able to rest. At that point, I had been wrestling with these spirits for about a month. Then one night in the dead of winter, I thought I heard my son, Xavier, enter the room. My sons were night owls and roamed the halls often. Sometimes they came to use my bathroom, so I thought I heard him come in. I felt something against my foot. My feet were out from under the covers, so it was possible Xavier was playing around with me in my sleep. My foot was hit again, and I came out from under the covers saying, "Why would you—"

I immediately was at a loss for words because my son was not in front of me. Instead, it was a grown man of Spanish heritage with slicked back black hair. He had this smirk on his face that I will never forget. Every time I think about it, it brings me to tears because this was a turning point in my life dealing with demons and spirits. I yelled out a blood curdling cry and put the covers back over my head. When I looked back up, he was still there. I jumped out of the bed continuing to scream for my life. It was a horrifying feeling. This man had to be real because he was still there! Xavier came rushing in to check up on me.

"What's going on?"

"There's a man in here!" I said. He could see the fear in my eyes.

"Ain't nobody in here Ma. See?"

I looked around the room. Nothing. He was right in that moment, but there truly was someone there before he came in. I was so shook that it began to make Xavier feel some type of way.

That next morning I had to call on the saints. Pastor Hazel came to my home and brought a prayer warrior with her. My father was still around at the time, and we all gathered in the living room. I looked up above the mantle at the large family portrait of Earl, myself, and our four children towering over us all. The devil wanted that picture burned to the ground. It was almost as if he was igniting corners of the piece little by little, melting the very frame it was in so it would eventually evaporate and no longer exist. We all prayed like never before in that living room. We prayed to restore peace in that house and for any spirits in bondage to leave. When we finished, Pastor Hazel asked about Earl.

"Is your husband in this house?"

"No."

"Okay. Well, the Lord told me to tell you that one of the women that your husband is with sent a warlock here to your home," Pastor Hazel said.

"What? We've been separated for at least six years. I don't understand why."

I hopped up off the couch and began pacing the room looking back at everything that had happened over the past month. I guess it all made sense. The warlock was that man who was in my room! The prayer warrior continued to explain.

"This woman sent a warlock here because she sensed you praying in the spirit. A wife's prayer is so powerful that the warlock came here to put the spirit of fear in you so you would stop praying for your husband. This woman has some type of magic that is holding your husband in bondage."

"A warlock? What even is that?"

"He's over the witches. A man in charge," she said.

My father and I looked at each other confused. What was going on?

"He was in my room. Pastor, please, can you go up there."

"No. I don't have to do that. Listen, you need to read Psalms 91, 23, and 103. Keep reading it. The spirit is gone, that's for certain. He will never be able to enter your home again. There is a hedge of protection over you in your life that we have prayed for here today. You understand?"

I nodded my head. I continued to read those Psalms for days following because she told me to stay grounded and rooted in the Lord reading those verses for 30 days. From that moment forward, I stayed consistent in my walk with the Lord. All the hurt and pain from my ex-husband melted away. I was fighting a demonic battle not only in my life but my children's lives because of some of the things Earl had gotten himself into.

Some years later, I was talking to him. He was no longer with that woman, and I could visibly see a change in him. He was better in more ways than one. I told him about what had happened years prior and what Pastor Hazel had said. Tears formed in the corner of his eyes. He began to open up.

"Years ago when I first met this girl, I gave her some flowers. Some years later, I was looking for something in her closet, and a box fell down. When I picked it up, those same flowers, brown, brittle, dead, came out of the box. Attached to the root of the roses was this red ribbon which was attached to a photo of me and her. I knew something was off about that girl, I just knew it."

"I prayed for you," I told him. His posture changed.

"I appreciate that, Tashera. I really do," as tears were falling.

I shared all of this to say that the devil really does what he can to attack you and your family, but he is after your marriage as well. Witchcraft is beyond real, but it was a higher power that brought me through it all. You have to bring God into it because you don't stand a chance against it alone. You may very well end up in bondage just like my ex-husband was. You may be a victim to a demon or spirit without the slightest idea that you are bound to something dark and disturbing. Your behaviors change. You change. But all that can be wiped away with one name—Jesus.

THE LESSON

THIS WAS A VERY humbling experience for me and brought me even closer to God. Let me give you some key strategies I learned to help you fight the good fight of faith.

When you have God, that's all you need.

One of the biggest challenges once you understand the spiritual realm is overcoming fear. When I first experienced a vision of my washing machine flooding, I didn't understand what was happening. When the warlock entered my room, I was scared. These events automatically caused me to have a sense of fear. Something was happening outside of my control. Although no one else around me saw it, I knew it was real. After finding out I had gifts and witchcraft was coming against me, I wasn't in awe but rather was nervous and scared. I was getting deeper with God and other entities were getting closer to me.

I was able to get through it by reading Psalm 23. It reminded me I had nothing to fear. I didn't need to fear evil witches and warlocks because God was there to comfort me. His hedge of protection was around me. The demonic realm could only come that close to me because I didn't know yet what I was dealing with and how to fight. Once I opened my bible and reminded those demons of what God said about me, they didn't come back.

Being on fire for God feels like flying.

When you spend time with God, it's life altering. The more I got to know him, the more my life changed. As soon as my feet touched the ground each morning, I knew I was safe in his arms. I knew I was fully protected and had a peaceful night's rest. Psalm 91 taught me to not be afraid of the terrors at night. God was all around me and my protection from all the demonic forces. Think of it as having a forcefield. God has this angelic covering surrounding you everyday. If you only call him, He will be there.

Trusting someone comes when you have seen their true character.

How can you believe in the demonic realm but not in God? You can't. As I grew in my faith, I trusted the Lord would take care of me. Reading Psalm 103 taught me the characteristics of God. His mercy is everlasting. As human beings, we get upset and won't speak to an individual again. We don't have the capacity for them to fail us. We aren't God. He forgives us and shows mercy. He loves us. I knew that no matter what evil tried to tear apart my marriage and family, God would always be there for us.

God, if you're really real, I need you to show up
and show me your power.

A lot of us have said this a time or two. It's our response when we have been believing for God to move in our life and haven't seen anything yet. When going through the process of my children and I losing Earl in our daily lives, my only option was God. I needed strength, and that was something only God could provide. The more I began to pray and fast, I realized I was tapping into gifts I didn't know I had. I didn't get on social media or talk on the phone. I went all in. I stayed in my bible, prayed all day, and drank only water. I turned down my plate as a sacrifice to gain clarity of the moves God needed me to make in my life. If you aren't ready for that, start with a few hours of water only and lead up to a day of water only. Take your time but know that fasting will be such a benefit.

However this kind goeth not out but by prayer and fasting.
(Matthew 17:21)

No matter what the world says, there are certain things that only prayer and fasting can break.

THE OUTRO

YOU CAN'T ALWAYS prevent fiery darts the enemy throws your way, but you can prevent total destruction by succumbing to the will of your Heavenly Father. It is God's will for us to be prayer warriors and to seek His face endlessly. We are to fall on our face and worship Him, surrender to Him. I had to and because I did, my children and I are still alive today. You have to remember to pray not only from your heart but your soul as well. Watch the Lord perform miracles in front of you.

We know that whosoever is born of God sinneth not;
but he that is begotten of God keepeth himself,
and that wicked one toucheth him not.
And we know that we are of God,
and the whole world lieth in wickedness.
(1 John 5:18-20)

Remember that as the verses in 1 John state, believers will not be victims of successful attempts from the enemy. We are covered. After Pastor Hazel came into my home that day, I walked down the halls of that home with my anointed oil and blessed it with every prayer and every scripture I could. It became a house of holiness, and the wicked would not stand.

THE AFFIRMATION

I will continue to walk in
the authority of the Lord
and His protection,
for no weapon formed against me
or my family shall prosper.

chapter vii

MONEY

I feel like what I put out, I got back.

Tashera Simmons

THE INTRO

WE KNOW THE BIBLE says the love of money is the root of all evil (1 Timothy 6:10), but what about the actual money itself? We need it to survive. Everything costs, and prices seem to always be going up. I believe the actual physical paper that we exchange goods and services for is not evil, although I've seen it used for the wrong things and placed in the wrong hands. I've seen it become a master to the people who worship it, people whose mouths water at the thought of it. I almost hate the very concept of it.

One thing is certain: I grew up with very little, and so did my ex-husband. The overnight success of his career led us to become millionaires in what felt like a nanosecond. Given the tribulations that came with that money, I'd trade it in a heartbeat. Those tribulations and tests, however, made me stronger in my mind and built my resistance to avoid falling into the tricks of the enemy when it comes to the dollar. Money is the one thing people claim makes the world go round. What money doesn't do is cause me to come out of character or betray who I love. The mighty dollar is consequently not so mighty to me. Hopefully I can help others take it off the antiquated pedestal it has been on for thousands of years.

THE STORY

WE WERE BOTH 27 years old when Earl's career kicked off and money started to flow in, truly blessing us like never before. The label offered to buy us a house. Earl immediately declined.

"I'll buy one on my own," he said simply.

That was that. We grew up dirt poor. Just because we all of a sudden had money didn't mean we had to blow it all on things of materialistic value. I remember when we met with the accountants for the first time. They wanted us to buy a bigger house in a more secluded area. We refused. We had a smaller house that we rented and in due time, when Earl got where he wanted to be, it would be up to him to decide if he wanted to purchase something with his own money. I agreed with him completely when it came to money. He used to tell me I knew how to budget my butt off! What we did not prepare for is the change to fame and fortune also changing so many people around us.

Earl and I became like fish in a tank on display for everybody to see, with people tapping on the glass erratically. Everybody wanted a piece. The money and the sudden fame became a powerful magnet sucking in any and all moochers. We came from such modest upbringings that it was an utter shock the way people who we had been around our whole lives were acting toward us. I determined then that money attracted the worst kind of people and could bring out the worst in good people.

As we began to hang around other celebrities, I noticed that was all who ran in those circles. Celebrities, not your average Joes. I didn't understand this concept before Earl's rise to fame but once I started noticing the change in the people, I understood. Celebrities hang around people like them because they get it, and they don't have to worry about someone being their friend just for money or recognition. Even after Earl and I broke up, some of the potential suitors I would go on dates with would question why I was even hanging out with them. I then considered the old rule of high-profile dating: "You never want to date someone with less money than you." I didn't care about that. I focused on being equally yoked with someone. Were we on the same level spiritually, mentally, etc.? That's what mattered to me. Financial factors did add up in the end, especially with men. Whenever a woman has a little more than a man, we know that story. I was categorized by men who were out of the spotlight as this person who only wanted to date celebrities. Imagine the difficulties of the dating scene back then, especially when the whole world knows your ex.

Money may not last forever, but love and good friendships can. Both are hard to find, so I'm very thankful for the friends that I have today. I feel as if what I put out, I got back. If Earl and I were anywhere near wealthy, it was best to keep it to ourselves for our family. I cringe when I see entertainers flaunting their wealth for other people, trying to make others jealous. This is what I meant regarding keeping it to ourselves. We did our best to stay humble. These rappers today want to wear a lot of jewelry and buy three different cars. We're living in a day and time where it is getting real scarce out there. People are actually in need on one hand and then on the other hand, there are people who worship money more than ever.

I remember when social media was becoming a thing. I would post where I was on vacation, just admiring the beauty versus showing off. I had one woman message me after seeing the post and say how lucky I was that I got to go on four vacations in a year when she barely got to take one! This was when I decided to be more private about the way I moved on social media because how things appear on the Internet is not always what it seems. People can get a false sense of who you are. People I didn't even know were messaging me regarding my vacations and other things I posted, so I started to realize that others really do count your dollars when you're on display, even though you don't have to have a tremendous amount of funds. Many people didn't even know that I had a job. This was information I kept to myself because it was my business, but I had bills to pay. I always had been proud of my independence as a Black woman, even all the way back to my first job at Burger King. People had all these ideas about where my money came from. Not once did they ever consider I could have made a way for myself.

With money comes jealousy and envy. Those spirits are some of the most disgusting to have, and they are not easy to shake off. They are truly dangerous. I don't have much experience with these spirits personally, but money is often the cause. The reason why Earl couldn't get some of the help he needed in the end was because of money. There were people who were just not being honest with him because of what they thought they could get from him. It's like fresh blood in the ocean. The sharks come hungry. Jealousy and envy will feed on you until you are unable to look at all there is to be grateful for in your own life. I know this because I've seen it eat people alive.

I learned so much at a young age when it came to budgeting. I was helping around the house with that first job because I was able to save. It doesn't take millions to feel rich. You can budget what you have. Enrich your mind, enrich your spiritual life, and watch wealth grow in your health, finances, and livelihood.

How can you glorify money as if it is bigger than you? Money serves you. It should work for you, not the other way around. All I can say is to trust God when it comes to money. That's what I learned. God over money any day! Realize He created the universe and everything in it. If you put Him first, your money will come. Whatever you want, it will come. Whatever you are supposed to get will be yours because God knows you better than you know yourself.

THE LESSON

MONEY IS ONE of the biggest issues society faces. Some feel like to be relevant or influential they have to have it, but that's not the case. I have learned a lot about the concept of money. Let me share my views with you.

People will not die to themselves because they would have to die to their money first.

That's the biggest problem I see with others. When they have to let go of their riches and trust God, they find it hard. If someone said, "Take off your clothes and run down the street naked for $10,000 or work hard for $10,000 for a year," many people would put their morals and values to the side for the quick dollar. Just as quickly as it comes, it goes. People are then only known for what they did to get the money, not who they truly are.

Trust God with your finances.

When asked to tithe one tenth back to God and trust Him for the other 90%, some won't do it. They feel they need all their money and can't afford to tithe. When you give God 10%, He will always provide even more than you could ever ask for. God blesses whatever you tithe. Trust Him. You were put into your mother's womb, and money wasn't swimming around in there with you. When you pass away, you can't take it with you. Enjoy the life God has given you and understand if you put God in the middle of your finances, everything will work out amazingly.

Money shouldn't be valued more than you value yourself.

When we think about money, we consider doing everything because of the cost. People work several jobs in order to take care of their family. You want to buy everything your child wants while some are just trying to provide for themselves. Growing up, my parents didn't mention money. I saw my mom and dad go out to work, but they never complained about what they didn't have or couldn't afford. We always had food to eat and a place to sleep. When I was married, we started off the same way. We were happy in God, love, and with our children. That was wealth for us. We had influence and impact because we helped our community before the fame that helped increase our reach so we could help even more people. Money at the end of the day is paper. We are the ones who put value to it.

Everything you think money can buy, God gives you freely.

This is why you need to die to yourself. The closer you are to God and the more you build a relationship with Him, the more your spirit rises and your flesh dies. Our flesh clings onto money, fortune, and fame. Our flesh wants to please others and be the center of attention. All of the things we think we need, we don't. We have all that we need. In the beginning, Adam and Eve had no clothing and free food from the land. We have created a society revolving around money. That was never God's plan for us.

For all that is in the world, the lust of the flesh, and the lust of the eyes, and the pride of life, is not of the Father, but is of the world.
(1 John 2:16)

God will give you all your heart's desires because He loves you. When you lust after money, you are in the world. When you die to yourself, you are in the spirit. Always remember that money isn't the answer. You will always be chasing it. God is the answer and can solve every problem you have.

THE OUTRO

PART OF DYING to self is killing off your fleshly desires. That includes greed and the love of money. If you die to your money, you can ultimately die to yourself and deny yourself all materialistic indulgences that do not go with you after you physically die on earth. This life is only a small fiber in the thread of time. When it is all said and done, you cannot take your belongings with you. Worshipping money or taking on jealous and envious spirits because your best friend bought the house you always wanted is never worth it.

Learn not only how to budget your money so you can have the life you deserve, but how to have a healthy relationship with it as well. You're in the driver's seat, not a piece of green paper. God made us humans to work AND glorify Him. He didn't create money to glorify Him. It can't do that, so why put it on a pedestal? If anything, lift God higher on the scales and see how lightweight money becomes. See how little material things will mean you. There's no greater power than God alone, and no amount of money or fame can buy that.

THE AFFIRMATION

I will receive God's undeserving favor
toward me as I see to it that
every dollar works for me,
and I am truly blessed.

chapter viii

HURT

I just remember feeling
this hole in my heart.

Tashera Simmons

THE INTRO

WHEN YOU WERE YOUNGER, can you remember the number of times you fell off your bike and bled from skin hitting concrete? Can you remember how many times someone said something unkind to you that deeply affected you? If you were to add up all the hurt you've ever experienced in life thus far, would it weigh the size of three persons or more like a cruise ship? Honey, let me tell you, you could add up cruise ships, elephants, the whole state of Texas, and sprinkle a few commercial airplanes in there, and it still wouldn't weigh enough for all I've been through.

The thing is though, it's not about quantity. One little incident could outweigh several others. I know the biggest upset I've had was my mother leaving me. That was some heavy stuff. It flattened and nearly broke me. There is a God who can help lift you up, dust you off, and fix all that was broken. Know that just like physical pain, emotional pain doesn't have to last forever. There is an ending, and the choice is yours as to when it will stop. That doesn't mean the memory of that pain won't come back and the trauma response won't be triggered. It just means you can shape how your body, mind, and soul recover, move on, and learn from it.

THE STORY

WHEN I WAS A KID, I used to wake up to Calypso blasting from my mom's record player in the living room as she sewed a dress for my sister. She was a beautiful seamstress. She'd just be singing along and smile wide as soon as she saw me walk in. She motioned to me. I had to be maybe 13. She did this often.

"Come, take the needle," she said.

So, I went to her and took the needle and began sewing the dress like she taught me before.

"That's it. Keep going."

I could smell breakfast waiting for us all. She was so happy, and so was I just to be in her presence. She was Panamanian, and she would often tell me stories about all the fun she had when she was younger before she had me and my siblings. She would talk about all the lovers she used to have. She joked and said she had a white liver, which means she had a very high sex drive in her younger days. I didn't really understand what she meant by that at the time. The way she talked about it was age appropriate as she shared exciting details, talking about a foreign land that was home to her and soon began to feel like home to me just from her retelling. She would try speaking to me in Spanish sometimes, and her dialect would always come through when speaking English. I admired her so much. She felt like a Saturday morning, a snow day, a summer break. Now that I think about it, maybe she was my first love.

By the time I was 14, my mother had made her very own carbon copy homemaker in me. The cooking, the cleaning, the sewing. We never had to buy clothes because she was always making them. The only thing we had to buy was shoes. At that age, I had been so on top of things as far as taking care of my siblings and myself that I wasn't babysitting as much as I used to. I could sense that I was on the cusp of something despite being locked in the house for years after the incident with my brother. Freedom was near, and I could smell it. It had a sweet aroma, and it was dang strong the day my mom let me go to the block party.

I remember the party was in Slow Bombs, a housing project area across town. Earlier that day, as I spent most of the morning trying to figure out my look, my mom was making me baggy pants because they were in at the time. To be really specific, they were Girbaud jeans that cost a lot of money. My mom found a pattern and made some because we couldn't afford them in the store. I mean with seven children, what choice did she have? I was happy that she had that going on. Meanwhile, I was trying to figure out my hair.

"I'm going to go to the store. I'll be back and finish up the pants!" she said to me as I focused on my hair in the bathroom mirror.

"Are they almost done?"

I checked the time. It was about 10 o'clock, so I still had plenty of time to get ready. My friend Kerry was coming to pick me up at 1 p.m.

"Yes. Almost done. I'll be back."

Off she went. She left to go to the store at exactly 10:30 a.m. as I recall. I was too distracted to see what all she took with her as she left to get her shopping done. Then 11 a.m. passed, then 11:30. *"She still hasn't come back yet,"* I thought to myself, hair done to perfection with what I had, shirt on, and staring at the unfinished jeans. I threw on some pants and I walked outside to see. The store is only at the corner. *"Maybe she went down to the one on the next block over."* I walked down to the corner and didn't see her, so I walked down to the bottom of the hill to see if maybe she went to the other one. Nowhere in sight. It was not like my mother to take so long knowing that I had something to do. She was making something for me, and she knew how important that moment was for me after a few years being imprisoned and trapped in that house. I went back home. My dad was out front. The summertime sun beamed down, and I shaded my eyes still looking back to see if my mother was behind me. Kids were playing and laughing just like I used to in the same grass.

At 1 p.m., Kerry came to pick me up. He was a really good guy friend and we were so cool with each other. He took one look at the pajama pants I was wearing and said, "Why are you not ready?"

"I was waiting for my mom. She was making me something to wear!"

I could tell if I took too much longer he would be annoyed, so I threw something else on. Although it wasn't what I originally planned, I thought I looked cute enough. Kerry and I made our way to Slow Bombs. The whole time we were walking and talking, I kept thinking to myself, *"What happened to my mother? Why didn't my mother come back?"* I couldn't wait to get back and find out why she took so long.

I didn't get back from the block party until 7 p.m. It was starting to get dark, and I could see the last little sliver of pink sinking in the far skies. When I went inside, I remember this eerie, airy feeling. It felt very empty. The kids weren't in the house. Normally at that time, my younger siblings would be in because mom would have dinner ready by then. It was dead silent.

I sat on the little porch and chatted with Kerry. It was then I verbally expressed to him my concern. My mother left around 10 a.m. and had not returned. Kerry played it cool. He wasn't fazed, and maybe I shouldn't have been. Surely she'd be turning the corner in her black burqa, returning from selling her oils and incense at any moment. She was a proud Muslim woman who sported the burqa often. I remember she had it on when she left for the store. I was so hyper fixated on getting ready that I didn't even remember hearing her haul the incense and oils with her. Time went on, and Kerry went home. I thanked him for such a good time. As soon as he left, the anxiety kicked in. My dad came walking up the block and I was happy to see him, so some of that anxiety eased. As I got closer to him, he reeked of liquor.

"Mommy left at 10 o'clock this morning to go to the store. She never came back," I said to him.

His facial expressions were emotionless, indifferent.

"What? Okay, all right then."

He patted me on the shoulder and stumbled into the house like it was nothing. Something wasn't right. I could feel it. I quickly made my way to my godmother's house, gathering my siblings because it started to get late. I got them prepped for bed. We lived in a railroad house so all the rooms were back with the kitchen and everything else in the front of the house. That next morning, I heard the commotion of pots and people talking. *"Thank goodness. Mommy is home,"* I thought to myself, and immediately got up to find out. I ran to the kitchen and to my disappointment, it was my siblings playing and my dad with a couple of his friends. He looked very concerned.

As soon as he saw me, he said, "Make your siblings something to eat."

"What's going on with Mommy?"

He said, "Everything's gonna be all right."

He was passive and dismissive to get me to do what I had to do. I remember at that moment a new feeling. I never knew what that feeling of hurt was, but it cut and was deep. It was unlike anything I ever experienced. It was worry, hurt, and fear combined.

I made my siblings breakfast, doing my best not to let my looks of disappointment and hurt show too much and spook them. I overheard dad telling his friends, "Let's check hospitals, morgues, jails, and parks."

They were coming up with strategic plans. I will never forget how my father looked because I'd never seen him like that. He was always this cool, calm, and collected guy. That night went by, then another night went by. Everything started to weigh on me with the absence of my mother. I had more responsibilities because my dad suppressed what was happening, which was so out of my mom's character. She was very family oriented. When I think about her, she was just very wholesome. How did she just disappear? Something had to have happened. She never really had friends beyond one in the building. She was very introverted. She stuck to her sewing, incense, oils, and my father. That was it. He thought somebody had killed her. Even her family got involved and flew up—her sister, mother, and father.

Everybody started getting involved on my father's side of the family too, including his sister and his mother. I just remember feeling this hole in my heart as if a piece of it was missing. My siblings began to cry out for her. The moment we found out she intentionally left was almost just as bad as if we had learned she was dead.

A few years prior to my mother's disappearance, she had gone to a funeral in Alabama on behalf of my father. He couldn't make it, so she offered to go and represent the family. Unbeknownst to my father, an act of adultery occurred between my mother and my grandfather. I guess from that moment on, she always had him in her thoughts. She carried whatever happened in Alabama over into her marriage to the point where it caused her to abandon ship and jump overboard.

Five years after the funeral and a few years after her disappearance, my dad's friend claimed she was spotted in New Jersey. My dad drove up there and went to his sister's house. To his surprise, his sister confessed to some unsettling news. Not only did my mom escape to Jersey to live with my grandfather, she moved in with the man in my dad's childhood home. They even kicked out my grandmother from her own home that she had built with her beloved. When my father told me this story, he had tears in his eyes. I had never seen him cry until then.

"Are you sure, daddy?" I asked sympathetically.

He responded, "Yeah. I went up there and seen them myself. They was in the house."

From that point on, I saw my dad lean on alcohol. He became a total drunk. All the hurt from the love he once shared was going down smooth with a bottle of bourbon. All those years my brother and I waited by the phone on the wall hoping it would ring and it would be her, she was with our grandfather. During those years, we were an afterthought. Because my father was so devastated, I had to mask my hurt. I had to stay strong for my siblings and keep them from freaking out too much as well. We have to unlearn masking because it causes build up. Painting on a smiling face when you are truly wounded is a tiring exercise. I would eventually give up the act and surrender it all to God.

THE LESSON

THE HURT YOU FEEL in your heart is a pain no one can understand. People can try to empathize with you, but they aren't in your shoes. I have been dealing with hurt my whole life and want to let you know, I get it. Healing is a process, and I want you to know you aren't alone.

*Your foundation, including who you are raised
and molded by, is so important.*

My mom always tried to be positive because my dad was always so stern. We had to stay in the house after my brother busted someone in the head with a rock. My mom saw the bright side. She made us feel like our home was an oasis and not a prison. She told us to learn different things to do inside. She was teaching us creativity and had us use our imagination. She always knew how to shift the energy with her spirit.

It's one of the traits I took with me. My mom taught me so much in a limited amount of time that I was able to care for others without her presence. In hard times, I was able to turn the situation around because I could see the green grass waiting for me on the other side.

This was also a downfall. Thinking of a person who brought you so much joy and who left without a word hurts. I didn't want anyone else to leave me. I threw myself into the family I had left. Something can be said about being the oldest. You feel a need to take care of others. The problem was, I was doing it for the wrong reasons. When people leave your life, it's okay. They left a situation. People aren't meant to stay forever. You are to learn the lessons from them.

You can easily find yourself pleasing others
to keep them from leaving you.

I had to change my perspective. I walked on eggshells for years. I wanted to be liked by everyone. I never wanted to feel the pain of being left in that way again. I had boundaries but didn't hold people accountable to respect them. Only after my father passed did I come to myself. I no longer care what people say or do about my choices. I'm going to live my life. I don't care how they receive me anymore because life is so short.

I let my past rule my future, and I had enough.

I should have never been a motherless child, but it made me who I am today. It was the deepest hurt I have ever encountered in my life. Now, as a mother myself, I would never intentionally leave my children in that way. I recognized what caused my harm and did the opposite with my children. You have to change and not create the same toxic behavior and patterns. I want to give my children all the love they can hold every day of my life.

Therapy taught me how to have healthy healing.

Although I have God and I know I can go to Him, I chose therapy, too. I found it so hard to fight the war of hurting. It controlled my life and how I felt rejection. When people walked away from me, I felt as if they were rejecting me. They weren't. They just had their own battles to fight. In hindsight, you will realize that some people leaving could be the best thing for you. We feel as if we can help everybody, but we can't. Sometimes you torture yourself keeping people around when they want to go. You have to know when to pray and let God cover them. It doesn't stop hurting, but you have to move on because there is so much out there for you.

The Lord is nigh unto them that are of a broken heart; and saveth such as be of a contrite spirit. (Psalm 34:18)

Remember even in your hurting, God is a friend to you. It's not always easy. There is not a simple way to overcome harm and discomfort when your soul aches but one day, you will wake up and it will be better because you will be different. Over time, you will see the pain has eased.

THE OUTRO

I WAS VERY ASHAMED about being left by my mom. I felt unworthy and damaged. I felt that I could never really be loved. I'm not saying just give it all to God and that's all you have to do. No. You have to go to therapy, too. You have to talk it through and get it out or the weight will just be too much. You have to do the work. My mother's absence after intentionally leaving us gave me abandonment and rejection issues that I carried and suppressed for so many years. My father's death unlocked it as well. So yes, hurt can resurface. It's not the same pain forever, though. Sometimes it is just the memory of the hurt that feels almost as painful. You have to trust that things will change just as I had to trust that I was going to be okay after my mom left. She eventually came back into our lives, and we took care of her when she got older. I had to fight through some of that same hurt that I was dealing with since the moment she left.

Are you still holding onto the hurt of your past so much that it is crippling you from your purpose? Are you not interacting with the one person who hurt you because you're afraid of the constant reminder of what they did? If your answer is yes to either question, I can say we have something in common. I've answered yes to both, but I realized how this one chance at life was all I had. If I was going to let anyone get in the way, why would I let it be the person who hurt me so many years ago? That initial hurt has passed. There is no need to keep torturing myself to feel it over and over again. That self torture had to die like everything else of the flesh. If not, it would have consumed me. We have an everlasting Father who will take on any hurt we ever go through.

> Cast your cares on the Lord and he will sustain you;
> he will never let the righteous be shaken.
> (Psalm 55:22)

Unstrap the chains of your childhood trauma. Cast down your emotionally abusive ex. Lay to rest your spouse who walked out on you. All of those things belong to God now. You don't have to carry them around anymore. That's where faith comes in.

THE AFFIRMATION

I lay my burdens and my hurt
at the feet of the Father,
trusting that my heart will be healed.

chapter ix

FΛITH

You cannot be in your flesh and
totally live in your faith.

Tashera Simmons

THE INTRO

SINCE MY EX-HUSBAND led me to Christ when we were young, I used to think that I modeled my faith in Jesus from Earl because it was so profound when we met. He truly walked in faith. But then, as I thought about my entire life, I realized that I had this faith well before him. Faith is belief in things unseen. We know wind exists. Do we ever physically see the currents that shift creating strong winds? No, but we feel it. We see the bending of branches and flapping of leaves. The same goes for God. We don't necessarily see Him, but we can feel Him and we can see how He manifests in our lives and the lives of others.

Not everybody has faith. It's something you can say you have, but only you truly know what you believe. I went on a journey of trying to find out how deep faith runs in people because I used to think that there was something wrong with me. I used to think that I was weird and using that word faith just to suppress something that I subconsciously did not want to deal with. Maybe you're struggling with believing in the unseen, the unknown, and are truly unable to trust God. It's something we all experience but when you have blind faith, it unlocks a whole different level of blessings that you're just not going to want to miss out on.

THE STORY

THE SIGNIFICANCE OF the number 14 can be similar to that of deliverance, spiritual perfection, etc. I think of the number seven—the number of completion, the number of perfection. Times that by two and you get 14. I think it's interesting that my mother walked out on me at 14, and then the same thing happened when my son was the same age with his father leaving the family. I looked at where he was in life, growing in height and manhood. Those feet were growing too. To be stunted by this roadblock and major obstacle would be completely tragic. This was when I had to pull together all the faith I had in me. I started spending more time with Pastor Hazel.

We met around the year 2000. Pastor Hazel was a good friend of my ex-husband. Earl introduced us because he was so taken away and amazed with her story. He set it up for us to meet. She did a 360 and turned her life completely around. She was known as a former big-time drug dealer from Yonkers who was leading others to Christ. She left behind her old life and became a pastor. When I met her, I was blown away by her authenticity. What I loved most was her humility. Her church was one of the first pentecostal churches I ever attended. There was a rawness about the place, and the love for Jesus there was so strong. Attending her church over the years has been something I looked forward to doing. The way her church worships God is like a rush! You feel the presence of God.

She began to guide me along a path that was good and pure. It wasn't perfect, but it had smooth ground and was solid. I was learning to walk upright and tall in the full armor of God. Pastor was surprised with the level of faith I had. We had to nurture it so it could grow of course, but it was there.

"You really do trust the process, don't you?" I recall her asking when we first met.

"I guess because I have no other choice," I said.

"No ma'am. It's a little bigger than that. You see, it's a gift that God has given you. I counsel people all the time, and they don't have the determination or the faith like you're demonstrating. You're determined to believe something more positive, something you cannot see. You don't know, it could be months from now, but you have this positive attitude in such a negative situation. This is something that comes from a higher power, not the way you move and think."

Understanding that my faith came from Him and not simply from the way I was built based on my response to situations in my life was a game changer. God restores our faith when we need it most. There's times when faith is low and we have to really dig just to believe, but He is indeed the source. Without Him, what is there to believe in? I remember looking at pastor and having this connection, knowing I could be open with her. We talked about having child-like faith. To be child-like is to be curious. To be curious is to be open to whatever God has to show or teach you.

A lot of people approach faith from this super, by-the-book devout angle that oftentimes misses the mark of being child-like. Children differ from adults in that adults have more knowledge about certain things. How in the world are Christians—whether Christians for more than 40 years or just a few—approaching their walk with God as if they already know it all? There's no way. I appreciate my pastor for educating me and encouraging me to have child-like faith.

The comment I made to pastor about not having any other choice but to have faith stemmed from times when I was so desperate that I didn't know what was going to happen. I felt that I had to believe or else I was going to crumble. This desperation and belief system happened so often that I felt I had this super power and that I could manifest anything. When I was a young kid, I used to imagine, *"When I get older, I'm going to do... and do...."* I used to feel as if I was a superhero. That was my way of trying to mend the hole inside of me. When I met Earl, we were on the same page. We were the "Wonder Twins" determined that we were going to manifest our life.

"We're gonna be rich! We're gonna be famous."

I used to say this stuff before I met my ex-husband. I used to dream when I looked at TV and thought, *"That's gonna be me one day."* Being abused verbally by my dad with him saying I would never be nothing but on welfare with children and that I was stupid and dumb was because he was an alcoholic. I didn't know it was the disease that was saying so many mean things to me, but I could have fallen apart. I could have succumbed to the things that he was telling me. But I was like, *"No, I'm gonna be better than that."* Everything he said was not true, and then I met my ex-husband.

Earl and I had the same mentality and the same attitude. We were broke from broken homes. Because my mother abandoned me, my father was verbally abusive. Earl's mother was also verbally abusive. We just knew there was more to life than what our parents put us through, and it was our faith that kept us going. But when Earl abandoned me and our children, that generational curse tried to creep in. I fell apart and went into a deep depression, but there was a small voice in me that told me to keep pressing on no matter what. I now know that voice was God! I grew up Muslim. I wasn't taught what faith really was, but I knew that there was something bigger. I learned more about faith in my 20s as I transitioned to Christianity, but I truly started to build an unshakable faith after the split.

Blind faith is believing without questioning things or having any evidence of something. For instance, truly believing that wind exists without any scientific evidence or seeing trees move or feeling wind gusts. That is blind faith. I even have a tattoo of an angel with her wings wrapped around my forearm. She has her hands over her face. I have her covering her eyes, and I have "Faith" in red underneath it. I put that there because it's a symbol of who I am and a reminder of how my faith has carried me through the worst times in life. I know how a lot of Christians feel about tattoos, but that's just me. Unapologetically Tashera. I often have to remind myself to look at that tattoo and remember why I put it there. I'll literally tell myself to pull it together and ask, "Tashera, where is your faith girl?"

Dying to self came in when I realized that all my traumas and tribulations have led me to die to my flesh and allowed my spirit to arise. You cannot be in your flesh and totally live in your faith. A portion of you has to die to yourself so that the Holy Spirit can have the strength to lead you in the darkest places in life.

THE LESSON

IT IS SO IMPORTANT to find yourself and know who you are. Following are some of the things I learned about faith in my walk with God.

Faith is on the inside of you.

In the beginning, I thought my faith was built within my ex-husband. I quickly learned I couldn't keep resorting back to him. I had my own life. He's a big part of it, but he didn't give me faith. I was always able to relate to him because of the gifts I already had inside of me. The problem is when you come up and are abused. It's damaging and makes you question trusting yourself. I had faith to believe my mother was alive after she didn't return home, and she was. Although it was years later before I found out, I never stopped believing.

You can't covet someone else's faith.

Once you begin to trust yourself, you begin to acknowledge God's voice in your life. Seeing someone else have faith to believe for things is great, but you have to believe for yourself. I can pray and want for someone to get a new home but if they continue to say they will live in an apartment, it won't happen. You can agree with someone in faith but not rely on them. You have to stretch your own muscles to believe. Trust that God will come through for you.

Even if you have been praying for years for a car and your friend received one overnight, don't stop. Your blessing is on the way. It will be something just for you. They may have been able to go to the dealership and purchase a car and you have to wait. The difference is God places it on someone's heart to give you a vehicle and it's debt-free. You had the faith for a car with no payment while they only wanted a car.

Faith is a mindset shift.

You cannot think on a lower level and have expectations. It doesn't work. You can't have faith in things but speak negatively. You have to hope for the things you don't have. See yourself with what you need. If you want a new home, keep yours clean and speak highly of your home. Don't always complain about what isn't working. Faith is knowing you aren't making enough at your current position, but you will be wealthy one day. Continue to work hard where you are and success will show up when you least expect it. Faith needs work. The position you are in could be the training ground for where you are going. It is teaching you the skills you need for the future. Now you have shifted from a poverty mindset to a prosperous mindset. Faith is at work.

Strengthen your faith in God.

I know you are saying, "Tashera I've been believing for a long time and I'm over it." Don't give up. This is when you have to build your strength in God. You can back up your faith with the word of God. Write down the things you are believing God for and back them up with scripture. Stop telling others what you want and talk to God. He's already working on it for you. When you start to waver, speak the word over your situation, pray, and God will show up right on time.

> *Now faith is the substance of things hoped for,*
> *the evidence of things not seen.*
> *(Hebrews 11:1)*

God orders our steps because if we walked where we chose, it would be a disaster for us. Remember your faith will produce evidence. He will answer our prayers. It may not be the way we want, but God always gives us what we need.

THE OUTRO

EARL HAD SUCH a great influence over me, especially with leading me to Christ. I felt that he was afraid to lose the most important thing in his life. We had a bond that was so tight, and I loved him with no conditions. It wasn't Earl, however, who instilled faith within me. It was God who restored my faith when I desperately needed it.

> *For it is by grace you have been saved, through faith—and this is not from yourselves, it is the gift of God. (Ephesians 2:8-10)*

We can't keep having the mentality that everything comes from us or other people. It's really easy to fall into that, especially when a lot of people in your life are willing to help you out in times of need. We must remember that God is the beginning and the end. With him, all things are possible. The opposite of faith is doubt. The blood of Christ, His unfailing love, is more than enough evidence to believe. If you take away all evidence and just have blind, child-like faith, you will find He is more than sufficient.

THE AFFIRMATION

I trust the process and will continue
walking by faith, not by sight.

chapter x

HIDDEN
STRENGTH

One thing I never detached from
was God.

Tashera Simmons

THE INTRO

THE STRENGTH OF an object is dependent upon many things. First and foremost, strength can be defined as an object's ability to stand against any pressure or force causing it to break or bend from its original form. You can see something and expect it to be strong but when you apply pressure, discover it's actually weak. The opposite is also true. Something thin and looking frail can actually turn out to be strong. Its strength is hidden behind false perception or a deceptive exterior.

I can honestly say that I discovered a hidden strength I didn't know I had. I know the devil saw it as a surprise. I may have looked as if I would snap under pressure, but there was something holding me together, pushing back against the very forces that had a power to break some of the strongest material. What was once hidden became unveiled, and nothing was going to shatter me into a million little pieces.

THE STORY

WHEN WE'RE CHILDREN, we're quite sure how we are built until we are up against the hardest challenges of life as we get older. When you're able to tap into a strength system that you had no idea of until unexpected trauma arises, you can see the framework for its origin. You can look back and remember every single thing that ever happened and begin to identify the moments where you showed strength you may not have recognized at the time.

After my mom left, I had to really step up my game. It was as if I had to take her place and become a mother of six at 14 years old. How could I show these little ones that everything was going to be okay when in reality, it felt as if everything was not? I remember muffling my cries at night over the abandonment I felt, the anger that was suppressed inside. Watching my dad fall apart and succumb to drugs and alcohol while I had to keep it together for my siblings was something no teenage girl should ever have to go through. Humans need structure and order in our lives, especially in those formative years when we are still coming up with how we feel about this very messed up world. There was no structure and no order.

While making ends meet at Burger King and helping my family the only way I knew how, there were other avenues I could easily have gone down. Someone offered me drugs. I can't quite remember what it used to be called. Although it was very tempting— and as a young girl, I was curious—I said "No." Something was telling me not to do it even though my flesh was very vulnerable to the things around me. The money was coming in, but we still needed more. Eight mouths to feed in one house. A few of my distant friends had been coming back with a good bit of cash. I would be so impressed and compare what I was making at my job to them.

"All you have to do, Tashera, is drink and have a good time. You won't even realize what's going on for real," one of them had said to me while trying to convince me to get on board.

Being an inner-city kid, it was easy to fall into what my distant associates were doing. Prostitution and stripping brought in a good bit of money from what I could tell, and I definitely considered it. But once again, something was telling me not to even go there. Although the temptation was very enticing, I decided not to sell my soul for an unbeatable price. I didn't care how much money it would have brought in. I ended up settling for jobs at ShopRite, Costco, and eventually General Motors. There was no way I was going to compromise. Little did I know, that was the hidden strength that God had placed within me.

My dad wasn't watching or disciplining me. I could have really done whatever I wanted after my mom left. I could've tried that drug that I was offered on multiple occasions. Everybody was doing it, and they seemed so cool, too. I used to see people smoking cigarettes and thought the way they could bend the smoke with their lips was so effortlessly dope. I even gave it a try by taking a smoke from my friend. She laughed at me as I coughed my little lungs out and nearly threw the cigarette a mile away. The taste of it made me feel sick inside, and I felt convicted even though it was just a cigarette. I had younger siblings watching me. How would I have felt if my brother, John, came around the corner and saw me coughing with a cigarette in my hand? I would have probably been a deer in the headlights. With no supervision, no oversight what-soever, it was as if God was this secret friend who had my back. It is a sad thing looking back on it. *"God, it's just you and me out here,"* I would think, realizing I had no one.

Growing up Muslim, I wasn't aware that the feeling I often felt, the spirit of conviction, came from the Holy Spirit. It was God trying to communicate with me, almost as if He was saying, "Stay clear from this, my child." He would then move me from one place to the next. Away from drugs. Away from prostitution. Away from having my body on display for any man to see.

When Earl started singing lyrics that didn't align with what I knew he believed as a man of God, I saw some of his strength fade. It was hard to watch. Some of those lyrics opened doors, and he brought some of those things into our lives. It was similar to those magical movies when someone would say stuff and it would happen. It was as if what he was rapping was coming alive, as if something was activated with every lyric he spoke. In one of his songs he said, "To live is to suffer." I really began to see that thinking take root, but I never detached from God. I saw how Earl had one foot in a secular world and another foot in a spiritual world. By watching his walk, I determined it was detrimental to be double-minded. We know that the Bible says a double-minded man is "unstable in all his ways." (James 1:8)

The hidden strength that I had within me all along was God and God alone. Without Him, I would have ended up in a different place. I more than likely would have sold my body for whatever I thought it was worth at the time, not realizing that I was purchased through Jesus's blood shed for me. The price had already been paid and for that reason today, I am free. I am free to do His will, free to be who He has called me to be. My strength is greater than that of diamonds, steel, and titanium. My strength is in the Lord and the power of His might.

THE LESSON

STRENGTH IS NOT always seen with the naked eye. Growing up the way I did took strength. Remaining to take care of a household when I saw the fast money and fun wasn't easy. Sometimes you don't know what you can do until faced with a difficult situation.

Examine your life with an objective lens
and identify what took strength.

To do this, I started therapy. I wanted to jump right into where I was at the present moment. My therapist suggested that I start from childhood, and I cringed. I wanted to know why that was the starting point. She said these simple words: "Because it's the beginning." We have to start with our foundation. I was hesitant about therapy at first, but it truly helped me build myself back up from being traumatically hurt in my childhood. I found myself in tears the first session, remembering all I had gone through. In the drops of water sliding down my face, I found where my strength lied. It was in me. The young Tashera who felt defeated still lives with me. The older Tashera was standing up to nurture and love the younger version of me. I was a protector of my family. It took strength to assist my family. I could have gotten a job and walked away, but I stayed. My love for them was a strength.

Stay the course no matter how enticing the other one looks
because looks can be deceiving.

Strength keeps you aligned to your destiny. There were so many places I could have gone and things I could have tried, but I turned them down. I grew up seeing first-hand the effects of drug and alcohol addiction. When it was in my circumference, hidden strength empowered me to say "No." As a teenager, I saw the bright side of money. The great thing was my parents already instilled in me not to value the dollar. I wasn't blindsided by what the world had to offer. I had the strength of discipline and hard work. I wasn't making much at my job, but I felt good about the way I made my money.

You can try and lean on your own strength, but know it will fail.
Strength has to come from God.

We are born with an inner-strength from God. When we try to do what we want based on our own image, we fail. As children, we don't know what we can do. As adults, we reassess what we have accomplished and how we were able to do it. As parents, we raise our children to not make our mistakes, but we need God's strength. I'm reminded of Samson who had strength given to him at birth by God. When he defeated his enemies, it was because of what God gave him. His downfall was telling a deceitful woman that his strength was tied to his hair, which had never been cut. He thought their love was strong enough that his secret was safe, but it wasn't. She cut his hair and God removed from Samson his physical strength. God sent a clear message that our strength comes through Him.

You can't have one foot planted with Christ and one foot with the devil.

I am always amazed at how I made it off of my block without mixing in with the wrong crowd. God covered me in my weakness. I didn't know what to do. It was the Holy Spirit keeping me from becoming a victim like those around me. I knew deep inside others were counting on me, and I couldn't blend in. I had to be uniquely different. Once I had a taste of who God was, I understood I had to be all in. I observed as people I knew tried to be with God and in the world. They struggled and would come back to Him, but the devil would have such a hold on them. God was always there, but they had to choose. The issue was they wanted the carrot the devil dangled, not knowing God had a whole farm for them. They didn't understand the enemy's offering would cost their soul.

For we wrestle not against flesh and blood, but against principalities, against powers, against the rulers of the darkness of this world, against spiritual wickedness in high places.
(Ephesians 6:12)

For six years, I could not stop reading Ephesians 6:12. I matured in my walk with the Lord and realized how real God is. His Spirit was real and it lived in me. There were things happening in my life that I couldn't understand but when I was introduced to Christ, everything made so much sense. Carrying God's spirit was all the strength I would ever need.

THE OUTRO

HOW STRONG YOU are has nothing to do with who you are but everything to do with who you pull your strength from. Do you ever think about some of the moments where you were weak and vulnerable and truly regret how you handled the situation? A lot of those moments come from us not relying on God to show Himself strong and intervene on our behalf. It's us folding inward about how something made us feel, curling into a ball to make ourselves small. We need to make ourselves big and uncover the strength within us that was hidden behind other things that got in the way.

Remember that there is healing power in God's strength. Don't compromise when you don't quite know if you can handle something because the truth is, you can only handle it with help from someone greater than you. I see human pride as something invisible that is hidden behind people who appear strong but are in all actuality brittle due to it. Whatever pride that you may have, it must subside. Humble yourself before the Lord and watch yourself become durable, unbreakable, and able to withstand any pressure or force attempting to misshape you from your original form that is perfectly imperfect—an original form more beautiful and stronger than it appears.

THE AFFIRMATION

My strength is from the Lord and
because He is for me,
nothing can stand against me.

chapter xi

SWEET LOVE

Their love is matched with God's love.

Tashera Simmons

THE INTRO

AS I MENTIONED BEFORE, I love all the different types of love. The sweetest love to me is that familial love, the love I have for my children and they have for me. It's sweet enough to get cavities and make your face scrunch up. Sweet, sweet love. It can be fuel for you to carry on through difficult times. I know it was for me. It ignited a spark underneath my feet to keep moving and aiming to be the woman God called me to be.

After my best attempt at a good marriage, I was left behind with four small souls. I had dealt with a common traumatic incident from my childhood. Those four little souls were one of the reasons why I was able to get over such a heartbreaking moment. There were moments of enlightenment just as there were traumatic moments that started me on my journey of dying to self. When doing so, there's always a newfound joy and appreciation for the ones who love you.

THE STORY

THE WINTER AFTER the separation was a harsh one. The house felt barren, the fridge near empty. I laid in my bed shivering because I couldn't afford to turn on the heat. My children came in to join me after my eldest helped them get ready for bed. I got up and plugged in the heater. My daughter, Praise, who was only 1 year-old, trickled in last. I picked her up and kissed her chunky cheeks.

"My sweet girl," I said to her as the others climbed into my bed.

This was our new nightly ritual to keep from freezing our butts off. The hum of the heater was becoming a comforting sound to all of us. At least I could pay for the light bill. That was a small win for us. Praise and I got in the California King that used to just host two instead of five. We had each other. We were still home, even though part of our home left us. He may have had his faults, but Earl was home to us. As I turned off the lamp on the nightstand, I didn't tell my kids goodnight. Instead, I felt the need to say something else.

"I don't know if you guys know, but Mommy was abandoned as a kid. My mom left us, and my dad went to drugs and alcohol so I had to take care of my brothers and sisters. It makes me really happy to see you guys being kind to one another and helping Mommy whenever you can."

There was stillness in the dark. They usually were a little antsy as we settled down, pulling covers every which way and what not, whispering when they were supposed to be going to sleep. I'm not sure if it was the tone in my voice or what I was saying, but they were silent.

I continued, "I don't know when your father's coming back, or if he's ever coming back, but he was very verbally abusive and we can't have that here. This is our home. We need to have peace here."

"We love you Mommy," my eldest Xavier said after a few questions from my 8-year-old about what the words "verbally abusive" meant.

I did my best to explain it, but part of me already knew that they understood what it was because they had seen and heard it themselves. Tears came down and I couldn't help the cries that continued to escape me. They all made their way to hug me, and we cuddled ourselves together to keep the cold from getting to us. As they fell asleep, I could feel the dried up tears on my face in the cold air as I looked at the ceiling.

I thought, *"God, I've been here before. This time it's only four kids. This is less of a load. Before it was six kids. I know you will make a way. I trust you, Father."*

I was able to recall becoming a parent for the first time as one of my boy's snores made me smile to myself. I was so scared to get it wrong, and knew I had to get it right. There was no choice, not after everything I had been through. Even when they were little, from the moment they started walking and making intentional eye contact with me, I would talk to them. I would be considerate of their feelings, but not in a way that would spoil them. I was very present and let them know, "I see you and I hear you."

I remember saying, *"Okay, God. I'm gonna make my own manual. Me and you are gonna make our own manual because you've been the one who's been guiding me."*

That manual was made with love. A lot of it was making it up as I went, but I made sure the felt tip pen was in God's hands. My son's snores brought me back to the cold, and I was extremely grateful to be with them at that moment. I may have been running out of money to pay the bills and keep the lifestyle we had maintained with Earl, but I never ran out of the love my children reciprocated. Because of that, I am forever wealthy.

One Christmas after things were starting to slowly get better emotionally, I told the older ones that there still was no money. I didn't know what presents would be looking like that year. I'm a big Christmas head and I like to go all out, so usually this would have hurt me so bad. But the beautiful thing about life is we have so many more Christmases to come. We had each other, and we were each other's gift. Instead of buying the most expensive toys on their list that year, we wrote letters to each other about what we mean to each other and how important it is to do life together. Being present and communicating in the storm of our lives, I was able to see how I had truly changed my kids for the better and how they changed me.

I didn't know what love was growing up. When I looked at my parents, I saw they cared for one another in the early years but as time went on, something shifted. My mom and dad used to say they loved me but after my mom left I thought, *"How could someone who loves me so much leave me so alone?"* So yeah, I was confused.

Just before Earl and I became official at 17, he was telling me he loved me. After I kept dodging him for months and months, the idea of love became a little more exciting. He used to show up to our house unannounced, beating on the door for me to come out. He'd intentionally go to places where he knew I'd show up. He'd ring my house door bell until he could get ahold of me, even when I wasn't at home. He truly pursued me, and I thought that was so interesting. Someone who was outside of the family, once a total stranger, could love me, Tashera.

"I love you and I want to marry you," he'd say often.

"You know you don't have to say that just to have sex with me, right?" That was my response.

He would just give me this look like, "Did you really just say that?"

What's sad to me is that I don't think he really loved himself. I believed he loved me but truly struggled with loving himself. His attention and his ambition to want to be with me was something I had never previously experienced. Although I ran from him for months because I thought he was not my kind of guy, his persistence prevailed. When I finally got together with him, you could feel the tension and the emotions that he felt for me. I would think to myself, *"Oh, so this is love, huh? This is what it looks like."*

Little did I know that the real loves of my life would come much later. At 21, Earl and I were two clueless adults with no idea of how to be parents, but were excited to say the least. My first child, Xavier, was an experience like no other. The adrenaline was pumping through my veins. Just the thought of seeing my baby boy's face for the first time was enough for me. I remember Earl stayed in the hospital room my entire three-day stay. We did it all together. Mommy and Daddy dinner, Xavier's circumcision, breast-feeding classes, the works. Once we took Xavier home, Earl did not leave his side. He did most of the babysitting while I went back to work.

Earl used to say all the time that having Xavier shaped his manhood, made him want to do more toward his career to be able to provide for a family of three. Me, him, and our baby boy. Then came Tacoma, our second boy. Earl would call him "mini me." In our home away from the noise of stardom and fanatics, Earl was able to be a normal person with his children on the floor in the living room playing with his toy cars with Tacoma and eventually Sean. In his eyes was the pure joy of family, life, and sweet seclusion—our own little bubble of happiness. When our baby girl came along, she was a promise to me that God would always be with me.

Your husbands and wives can leave you but truth be told, the ones you birth into this world won't deny you. To this day people tell me, "You raised good kids with these good hearts," and I agree. I did indeed. Everything that I wished for and ever wanted as a kid, they are doing to me. There's times where I want to rough them up a little because they are not doing what they are supposed to do in school, but I don't because it's nothing too much. I couldn't have asked for better kids.

On the other hand, my dad was a gossiper. He had a bad upbringing, so he was really into divide and conquer. He tried that with me and my kids when he moved in with us to help me out with driving the kids to school and wherever else I needed help in the house. We would have talks where they would say, "Grandpa told me that your food wasn't good today and that you coming in late trying to cook was ridiculous." He would just be talking all this junk about me, and I would confront him.

"So, what you say?" I'd come up to him while he was in the kitchen, my kids peeking behind me.

"Mmhmm, grandpa. You in trouble," they'd say.

You best believe he would never be able to divide us again. After a while, he saw that and the love me and my kids had toward him. In his last years he told me, "Thank you for allowing me to see what healthy parenting and children look like."

This truly shook me. It was a gift, considering he always had something to say. For the last 10 years of his life, he had been clean and dedicated himself to his family in a way he had never been able to previously.

Today, I look at my kids who are grown. One of them is living in California in his 30s. How blessed am I! My youngest is 19. She, my son, and myself go to the movies every Friday, even if it isn't a good movie. We go to dinner on Saturdays. I often ask God what I do to deserve this, but I stop myself. I followed His plan. I picked from my childhood what I did not want to do and did it differently with my own children. Their love is matched with God's love.

One of my old therapists nine years ago told me, "I just want to give you a wake-up call. Your kids will get older, and they will leave you. I remember this story about a 91-year-old woman who gave her whole life to her kids. In the end, that was her biggest regret because she wound up being in her 80s and alone."

I was upset when she told me that. I never went back to her and got a new therapist, but I always kept that in mind. It is true that our children get older and need to live their own lives. It's not so much they're gonna leave us, but they have to have their own lives. I always kept that in mind and made sure they did what they wanted to.

If they wanted to go away to college, I told them, "Go live your life. Do whatever your heart desires! Don't worry as if Mommy's gonna be by herself because at the end of the day, I know God has a plan for me."

I did my job raising them. If they wanted to go out into the world, get married or whatever, who was I to stand in the way? I wanted to make sure they instilled that same kind of parenting as they went on to have children of their own so that I could keep this good generational trend going—a generational blessing rather than a curse. "Grandma will be taking care of your kids. I'll have my own man. I'll have my own life going on." I would tell them this.

But I had to go back and see where it all started and what kind of love I was receiving that made me want to be this person who no matter what other people do, I'm always trying to show love even if they don't reciprocate. What were my original ideas of love, and what was the ideal love that I should be receiving? The ideal love was the one I was receiving from my kids. That was it. That was all I needed. All the fake love from everybody else was irrelevant. These were the types of things I'd discuss with my new therapist.

When my eldest son came to visit me one summer, I shared with him that I was happily single for real. He was so happy for me, and we just opened up with each other. I told him I had been celibate for 10 years. This was the same son who walked in on me screaming in horror after seeing a warlock/spirit in my room, the same boy who heard his father yell foul things at me in front of him. He was the one who helped me pay my lawyer bills after the mistresses and baby mamas came for everything, and who refused to take a dime from me when I tried to repay him. My boy was proud of me, and I was proud of him.

THE LESSON

LOVE IS A VERY interesting word. Some people misunderstand or abuse it. I allowed it to flow through me, and I am able to see the manifestation of it in my children. Following are a few things I learned about love.

Let those you love know that they are important period,
not just to you.

Love is to be freely given to others. I have been able to share it with so many people, and my life has been touched by it. When love is abused, people are made to feel as though no one else loves them or ever will. People become bound by a prison of love. You may have heard of the statement, "No one will ever love you like me." People who say that want the person to feel unimportant to others. This is very untrue. There are plenty of people who will love you. Love is definitely an action word. It is seen in how you smile, speak, hug, and a host of other ways.

Healthy love brings joy.

I loved someone before I understood the emotion. I based love on what made me feel good. In my youth, it was a young man who pursued me and always let me know he cared. This situation caused me hurt in adulthood because I confused pain and pleasure with love. As an adult, I grasp the realization of love. It brings joy to my heart. It's not about a person but what I carry on the inside of me. God is love. Every time I come into contact with someone, I express it. I give them the experience of meeting the God I know in the way they receive love from me.

Children are sponges for love.

As adults, children listen to everything. While in the car, they are listening to the conversations you have with them and others. Although they are not responding or communicating their point of view, they are taking it all in. Children need to feel loved even though while they are young, they don't know how to ask for it. Spend time loving them. They have a voice and a mind. They are learning and hearing from you. Don't look past small children because they are young. One day they will become big like you and me. What you put inside of them will return back to you.

Perfect love is what we should be aiming toward in our lives.

We are all searching for the perfect love in a marriage. If we don't find it there, we search for our children, family, or friends to love us unconditionally. When they fail to meet our standards, we become upset and want to give up on love, but they were never meant to be that love for us. The perfect love we are seeking can only be found in God. No human being is perfect or ever will be. We were created in the image of God but not as Him. It's inevitable we will make mistakes because we live in our flesh, but that doesn't mean we can't love. Our purpose is to love as much as we can for as long as we live just as Christ did. Even in our hurt and shame, we apply the patch of forgiveness. Love teaches us how to let go when wronged in a situation and to move forward with forgiveness. Love sets boundaries to protect our heart. Love acknowledges when we are wrong and resists pride to admit it. Knowing God sent Jesus to die for your sins—that's love.

Perfect love casts out fear.
(1 John 4:18)

Don't be afraid to love. It's instinctively inside of you. When you first love God, you will then know who you are. Learning to love the way God does is the true way to make better choices in life and relationships.

THE OUTRO

FIGURING OUT THE MEANING of love was the ultimate thing that I needed to do to be able to survive in a world that is so uncertain and filled with unexpected behaviors. This was the only way I could truly thrive the way God wanted me to and die to myself. Any confusion of what I thought love was supposed to be was resolved when my kids came into my life. Love is everything, and God is love.

If we remember Jesus's love for us, we can let it be *shed abroad in our hearts* (Romans 5:5). Sweet love can shine through us and before men and women who know nothing of God's perfect love. When you feel the need to scream at the top of your lungs at your spouse or cuss out your sister for something she didn't do right, ask yourself, "Do I love this person?" If the answer is "Yes," proceed with caution. If what you're doing is stemming from the opposite of love—hate or even worse, indifference—you need to re-evaluate. Sweet love doesn't fade. God's love is eternal.

THE AFFIRMATION

I allow God's love to shine through
and understand that love is not just
a feeling but a choice to show God's
grace and mercy toward others.

chapter xii

CELIBACY

Love from another man, or any man,
wasn't the love that I needed to heal.

Tashera Simmons

THE INTRO

A FEW YEARS after my ex-husband left me and our children, I found myself fighting for my life. Soul ties are a thing. We have to be careful who we create that special bond with, which is a truth I learned the hard way.

There's nothing like being hot and heavy with someone in an intimate space with two bodies gravitating toward one another. I found that my reasons for intimacy went beyond instant gratification and attraction. When dying to self and killing the flesh, giving up sex absolutely transforms your outlook on life. Lust is something we all feel at one point or another. Evading it can seem almost impossible, and then not acting on it can be even more difficult.

Choosing a path of celibacy has to be a decision made for the right reason. If not, it will be easy to falter. Even if you can't make a long-term commitment to being celibate, I highly recommend trying it out. God will reward you for being faithful and determined. Following His rules and laws as stated in the bible will bring you closer to God.

THE STORY

CELIBACY AFTER NEARLY 30 years of friendship, marriage, and loyalty with my childhood sweetheart from the age of 17 was scary terrifying. He was all I dedicated my whole entire being to. I was out of the game for so long that I had nothing but questions: What is dating? How do I even date? What does dating look like 30 years later? I didn't even know if I still had it. I felt lost in a sense and ashamed.

I remember Earl saying, "No one would wanna date DMX's ex-wife." Talk about planting an insecure seed! *"Was this really true?"* I thought to myself. Five years post break up, I needed to take some time to heal before allowing another man to lay on top of me. Without totally being educated on sex and the effects of what it brings into a relationship, whether you are committed as boyfriend and girlfriend or just having sexual intercourse for fun, I found there is a whole other layer deeper than I ever knew.

In the interim of my healing before dating, I was working on my spiritual growth and entering a newfound relationship with Jesus

Christ. Digging deep into the character of God and His laws stated clearly in the bible, I had a lot of internal conflict because the word talks about adultery. It's a sin, however, for some reason I was still attached to my ex even though I was no longer involved with him sexually. It was like a part of me was still yearning for him in my flesh even though I knew I couldn't be with him after everything that had transpired. Why was that? I wondered how this could be after all that had happened. The more I dug, I learned the purpose of sex after marriage in the bible. Sex is not just sex regardless of how into the act you are with your partner. It's more. It is a union of two people and creates a soul tie.

In my post-marital love life, my first sex partner was a therapist about five years my junior. I didn't want to date anyone in the entertainment business. He was attentive, handsome, tall, and he was Panamanian like myself. We got along very well from the beginning. Afraid to give myself to him too soon and not knowing what I was doing, I treaded lightly. To my surprise, he was very patient, and I think even happy to be sharing the company of the ex-wife of DMX. During 30 days of dating, we had great conversations, great food, and an amazing sex life! I was experiencing feelings I had never felt before. I felt liberated with no commitment, just sex and freedom. After a year of dating, I noticed he had quite a drinking problem. Because I dealt with a man with those issues in my previous marriage, I knew the signs and ran as far away as I could.

My second sex partner was someone I knew from my past who I had a crush on when I was younger. He was a businessman and entrepreneur, sexy with charisma. He came into my life as a real kind and caring gentleman willing to financially support me and take me on trips. He was amazing in the sheets. I really couldn't get enough of him. After a solid year, I noticed his interest in my business and the entertainment world became his number one priority. He began asking to come to meetings with me, wanting to partner up with me in business deals and wanting to invest. I found out he was trying to go behind my back with one of my good friends who was a producer to create his own show. I think you can figure out the rest. He was an opportunist. Unfortunately, it comes with the territory.

After the opportunist, I was very turned off. I decided I needed to take a break in dating and start to really try to work on myself. My third and last sex partner came into my life when I least expected it. I was not interested in dating at all and contemplating celibacy, looking to finally focus on God and me. As I sat in a restaurant on 125th Street in Harlem with a few business partners, there he was walking down the street. He looked like a chiseled statue in his construction worker uniform.

A woman business partner said to me, "Jesus, he's fine! He looks arrogant, though."

"Well, let's find out. Do you want me to try to hook it up with you two?" I said to her.

"I dare you."

I walked up to him and said, "Hey, handsome. What's your name? My girlfriend thinks you're cute."

He responded with his name despite being a bit taken off guard and said, "There's one problem. I'm not interested in her. I'm interested in you."

"Me? Really? And why is that? You don't even know me."

"The fact that you have that tattoo on your arm is why I want to get to know you more," he said pointing to my Jesus tattoo on my shoulder.

We sat at that restaurant for four hours talking about life, Jesus, and relationships. To be totally honest, I fell in love with his spirit from the moment I sat with him. He didn't watch much TV, so he didn't know who I was and who I had been married to. He was a God-fearing man with a kind and caring heart who had no agendas or motives. He was very secure in who he was and who he wanted to be with. It felt so good to be with someone who didn't know anything about my past and wanted to get to know me for me.

For the first time in a long time, I felt normal and secure with someone. We went to water parks. We did picnics in Central Park. We laid there for hours talking about everything good. It was really too good to be true. He was the first man that I introduced to my children. I saw the love of God in his eyes when he looked at me. I could feel how much he cared about me. What I learned in that friendship and from the love that he projected to me was how to be in a healthy relationship. Still needing to heal, I ended up sabotaging the relationship subconsciously. He was a few years younger than me and was eager to go out and do things like having fun beach days and road trips. All I wanted to do was have sex.

He would say, "What do you want to do today?"

I would say, "Let's just stay in bed all day and have sex."

He would go with it but after so many times of saying that's all I wanted to do, he one day turned to me and said, "I love having sex with you, but I'm starting to feel like that's all you want."

What kind of man wouldn't want a woman who always wants to have sex? Surely something was wrong here, right? Alarm bells started ringing. Maybe there was something wrong with me. Why did I always crave sex so much? I realized that I had a sex addiction. He was right. Maybe all I did want from him was physical. His strong, kind, caring, and loving mannerism toward me started to make me angry. It started to make me see myself and my brokenness. Some people use drugs and alcohol to cope, but I found that I was using sex to suppress my pain.

I began to do research and found out that sex can be a tool, a coping mechanism when undergoing life changes or traumatic events. I continued to sabotage the relationship. He had no idea what was wrong with me or why I suddenly started being so distant even though all he showed me was love. It was a sad realization for me. I was tired, I was lost, and I realized that I was going in the wrong direction. Love from another man or any man wasn't the love that I needed to heal. It was God's love that I desperately needed.

One day before going to see my man, I prayed to God, "Am I really suppressing my hurt and pain with sex?" As hard as it was to ask God this question, it was more arduous to say, "If this is what I'm doing, take it away from me. Take every urge in my body and mind for sex. Allow me to lose the lust for it." When I and this guy had sex for the last time, I felt dirty and disgusted in a way that I had never felt before. At first, I was upset with God for doing what I asked. "Why, Lord? It just feels so good," I would say to him.

I truly heard Him say, "Does it really?" He didn't need to say anything else. It's like when you can see the expression on someone's face and already know what they want to say to the point they don't need to speak. God spoke and I could just imagine the look on his face. He needn't say anything else.

I asked God for one year and to date it has been 10 years sex free! Being celibate has been the most rewarding journey I have ever been on. The first two years, I had to cleanse and detox from every soul tie, every person I had sex with. That's when the power of God stepped in, and I began to feel the Holy Spirit. My prayer life became more powerful. My relationship with God became closer. God's voice became louder. I started to manifest my whole entire life into fruition. I would fast in power and speak into people's lives. I was casting out demons and warlocks. I traveled to Israel to the Jordan River and was baptized. In that river, I felt the warmth of Jesus Christ move from the tip of my toes to the crown of my head. I am forever grateful for choosing God over my flesh. My soul is free, and I have been made whole again. There is healing power in preserving yourself for the Lord.

THE LESSON

BEING CELIBATE for years has changed my views on many things. If this is the path you are on or thinking about following, here are some breadcrumbs for you.

Identify what tempts you and stay clear from it, or you can find yourself compromised!

If you have to yell "stranger danger!" at a fine man who comes up to you in the grocery store because you know you are a sucker for fine men in grocery stores, honey, do what you must! Celibacy is one thing you have to be disciplined for. No one is there to pull you out of a person's bed. You have to set up boundaries for yourself. Don't go to someone's home if you know you can't contain yourself. Your best friend could call you and tell you to leave but you won't. There is a place inside of you that thinks you can handle it this one time, but you know you can't. It's hard when the temptation is so easy. The old saying, "You can't have your cake and eat it too" is true. Once you eat it, it's gone. You can't touch and caress and think it won't lead to other things. Take your time and don't set yourself up for failure. No one knows you better than you know yourself.

Eliminate the perfect entrapment of distraction.

Temptation is not your friend. The donut glimmers from the glass case so brightly after you make the decision to lose 10 pounds. Sex is the same way. You decide to keep yourself and someone comes around who seems to be exactly what you are looking for. They have the voice, the look, everything you want right when you have called off sex. Don't fall for it. Distractions can fall under the umbrella of what you watch and listen to also. Do not watch or listen to anything with too much sexual content. We have to continuously be conscious of what we let in our eye gates and ear gates. Being aroused can lead you to make impulsive decisions that are regrettable later.

Remain focused on your celibacy journey. Don't entertain anyone or anything until you are in a place where you trust yourself. It may seem to be a great situation, but it can cost you the time you have invested into creating a healthier you.

Be careful of the ties that bind.

Celibacy is one of the best options to choose. Truthfully, waiting until you get married is best but if that wasn't your story, you can begin again. Waiting is a long but fulfilling choice. You gain more clarity when you are not clouded by sex. Once you meet someone and have sex with them, a soul tie is created. It produces a covenant with that person. You wonder, "Why do I feel like I can't leave this person alone when I know they aren't good for me?" It's because you have bound yourself to them with sex. You used to go on dates and learn about one another, now you don't. Some people end up marrying a person to only find months in that they have absolutely no business being together. You start to remember how you ended up in such a situation. Sex.

Remember that you have the power to choose this path,
and it is NOT for everyone.

Learning this truth changes a lot. When you have been in an unhealthy or toxic relationship, it's sometimes easier to become celibate. For those who have never had any issues, you may not see the fullness of living a celibate lifestyle. Celibacy is not just about lacking sex but rather becoming your best self. It is making wise decisions and following the path laid out to you before God. I know what you're thinking and no, I don't want you to become a nun. There is plenty of time for sex later in life with the right person at the right time. Celibacy is not an option for the weak. It seems the whole world is one big promotion of living a sexual lifestyle, but you don't have to cave in to it. It's okay to be different. Don't worry about what other people think of your decision. It's not for them. Don't let anyone deter you from doing what is right for you.

Watch and pray, that ye enter not into temptation: the spirit
indeed is willing, but the flesh is weak. (Matthew 26:41)

Our flesh is always what pulls us into dangerous places, but God knows how to get us out. Trust that you have made the best decision. Let me be the first to congratulate you on your new course.

THE OUTRO

CELIBACY SAVED my soul. I know some readers won't be happy to know that choosing celibacy is empowering. Sex is so tough to give up, I know it. How can you quit something that just feels so good? Getting a facial also feels so good but if you got one every day for the rest of your life, harm would come to your skin. Eating ice cream feels so good for the soul but if you eat too much of it, you'll get sick. Basking in the sun feels so good but if you were to stay in the same spot outside for the rest of your life without ever stepping out of the sun, the rays would do irreparable damage to your skin.

Just because it feels good doesn't mean it is good for you. God intended sex for men and women who are in covenant with one another because of the deep soul bonds that form and the purpose He has for us to be fruitful and multiply. I'm here to tell you that choosing celibacy was life-changing for me. I am a powerful woman of God because of it.

My purpose in being totally vulnerable in this chapter about celibacy is for you to prayerfully see yourself through my story and journey of dying to self and to make your life easier.

THE AFFIRMATION

I will preserve my body as a vessel
for the Lord and come against any
temptation that may sway or distract
me from a path of celibacy.

chapter xiii

LOYALTY

If you choose to be loyal to a fault to
humanity, then stick to that because it
all flows from God.

Tashera Simmons

THE INTRO

THINK OF THE PERSON most loyal to you at this moment in time. Do you trust her with your life? Do you show him that you value him? Do you reciprocate that same loyalty in return? Loyalty is an allegiance and consistency in the way you show up for someone. It's big "ride or die" energy that is so rare to find. I'm lucky to say that I've known a few loyal ones that I could always count on. The big question is, are you a loyal person? How do you keep from blurring the lines between that which is loyal and that which is people-pleasing?

Something that I am continuing to kill off to this day as a 53-year-old woman is people-pleasing. It's just some fat that needs to be trimmed. As I have been attempting to do this over the years, I've found that you have to let go of a lot of expectations. You may be a people-pleaser. You may be loyal, but you shouldn't expect the same from the people you please or the people you're faithful to. Dying to self includes killing expectations of others by accepting the expectations you have for yourself since it will always and forever start with you.

THE STORY

AFTER YEARS OF DOING and doing for others, the Lord opened up my eyes to this horrible habit of people-pleasing. I found myself doing things that were beyond my abilities just to make someone else happy. Given I wasn't happy myself, why in the world would I be so driven to be the source behind someone else's happiness? It doesn't make sense if you truly think about it.

I remember reading a story about a woman who had nothing but gave everything. Let's call her Rosie to protect her privacy. She was a CNA and worked the night shift. She had no kids and was the eldest of a big family. She had a friend who she had known since birth who was really struggling to find a place to live after a nasty break-up, so Rosie let her friend and her two kids move in. She gave up her own bed for this lady and her children. Whenever they needed food, she'd buy plenty for them even though they'd eat it all within days. Whenever they needed to go to karate practice, work, school, or church, she used her beat up Cadillac to take them. She'd even let the friend use her car on occasion and would catch a ride with some of the other nurses when it was time for her to go.

On top of all of this, Rosie's mother started needing help at home after falling down some stairs. Her siblings begged her to help take care of their mother even though they could have done it themselves. Maybe it was the fact that she was a CNA, I'm not really sure why they wouldn't help out poor Rosie. She'd drive that banged up Cadillac and take care of her mother during the day when she should have been sleeping in while her friends and the kids were at school and work. She'd follow this schedule day after day just to barely get any sleep, help, or time to herself. Her boss ended up asking her if she could stay longer at work after someone went out on maternity leave. Rosie said yes. She made it work.

She got in a car accident one day after leaving her mother's house. The car was fine, but she was in constant pain. She pushed past it and kept on. When she got home, she found that the friend who had been staying with her had wiped her out. She took the stash of savings Rosie had hidden and pretty much robbed her of everything. Rosie came to the point she was so tapped out that she attempted to end her life. All she ever did was give and give and give until she had nothing else to give. Her loyalty to her friends and her family almost cost her life. Thank God Rosie made it out alive. Her attempt was not successful and she was able to have a new outlook on life.

If you've ever felt like Rosie—like your devotion to other people's happiness went beyond just being a loyal individual—we are the same. I have some situations that I can't go into because I don't want to put anyone down or come off as if I'm just talking myself up about how loyal I am but trust me, I understand the Rosies of this world. I had to learn to be loyal to myself first and to God. A long way down the road, I learned that the only person who is going to truly be loyal to me is God. But I had to start with me first because He lives inside of me.

Let's go ahead and say there is no loyalty. It actually doesn't exist. If you come across one or two people in your lifetime who truly love you with no conditions, are loyal, and who take their friendship toward you seriously, then you have found a gem. Outside of that, it's almost as if it doesn't exist. It can, however, exist within us. I realized that we are all individually one person, yet we are also our own person. You have to understand that what you give out is not going to always come back. Whatever you do in life, if you choose to be loyal to a fault to humanity then stick to that because it all flows from God. But never expect someone to be loyal to you to a fault because that's just not gonna happen. When you are disloyal to yourself, that's when you should be concerned. To be real, every time you fall into that people-pleasing habit, you are being disloyal to yourself.

For some people, loyalty is just a word but for me, it's more than that. It's about being dependable. It's about feeling safe and finding comfort with that person you can trust with anything. I know that I can always count on them, and that for me is huge. I feel like dying to myself really taught me that because when we die to ourselves and live in the spirit, we see people for who they are.

Today, I mostly find myself being loyal to my children. I thank God they have been steady and loyal to me no matter what. It's important to be truly loyal to yourself first, but I'm grateful in all those times that I really poured out my loyalty to my children. I've had my Rosie moments before but when it comes to me children, they are my life. I still make sure I have that balance though and pour into myself.

In my journey, I've also uncovered that the opposite of loyalty is jealousy. From baby mamas to even some family members and total strangers, I've seen how jealousy can manifest itself. Pastor Hazel used to say to me, "You can give someone a whole cake but then forget to give them the last slice left. All they will remember is that one little piece that you didn't give them." Pastor was absolutely right.

My dad wasn't perfect, but he was loyal. Money and influence can change loyalty for sure, and in the worst ways possible. People you thought were for you will flip on you and come for you. The biggest lesson I learned after my father's death was that I had to practice being loyal to myself. I had to put myself first. How can you just allow yourself to put other people before yourself? It's a constant disservice to yourself. There's a difference between being selfish and putting yourself first. Selfishness is when you act as if you are the only thing that matters always, whereas putting yourself first is just switching the order of which things matter.

THE LESSON

WHEN YOU THINK of loyalty, it's normally associated with a person who is consistent in showing up or something that never lets you down. You expect that will never change. As you think about loyalty, consider the following ideas.

Sometimes, family can be the worst ones when it comes to being loyal, but you love them anyhow.

Let's start with having loyalty within a family. Your family is what you were born into, but relatives are normal human beings with their own emotions and feelings. They are not created to necessarily be your best friends. Many try to build this close dynamic with parents, siblings, cousins, aunts, or uncles. Sometimes it works. You see people who always hang out with their favorite cousin or aunt, but it's not for everyone. We are all built differently. You watch the Hallmark movies with the families gathering for the holidays and see how far-fetched it is from your real life. It's okay. We are all raised differently. The best thing to do is when you see disloyalty, let it go and come to an understanding that your family member will not be loyal. If later in life they become loyal to you, great! If not, don't get depressed or upset. People show you who they are and we get upset because they aren't who WE want them to be. Relatives will always be family but that doesn't mean they have to be your friend.

You may not be able to scratch your own back,
but you can have your own back.

How can you trust someone to be loyal to you when you aren't loyal to yourself? You tell yourself you are not going to cheat on your diet but you do. You are never going back to the coffee shop because all of the staff was rude to you, yet a friend suggests it and you find yourself there, rolling your eyes as the staff runs to serve your friend. As soon as one person invites you to a party and flakes on you, you are upset. They are only doing to you what you have done to yourself over the years. Have you found yourself complaining about a situation and then someone close to you treats you the exact way that was upsetting? Why? They feel as if you allow someone else to do it and never say anything so you will be silent with them also. Treat yourself the way you want others to treat you. Be loyal to yourself first and others will follow your lead.

Business relationships can feel like trying to break a rock
with a feather as your tool.

When you have a business, you need to have loyalty. Employees need to want to work for your company and not jump ship at the next opportunity. You need partnership loyalty with people who will invest time and resources into your ideas and not steal them. Loyalty is needed all around you. You must identify what loyalty looks like to you. Some people work with anybody, but don't let that be you. Work with someone who is aligned to your values and your vision. The characteristics of business loyalty are commitment, trustworthiness, longevity, and support. You need a team that can run without you but has your best interest at heart. Guess what? If you haven't found a team such as this, create it. Be the business people are busting down the walls to work with. Become what you don't see. Don't stay connected in places below you because God is always for you.

Without God in your life, your loyalties will always be divided.

The only person who will always be loyal is God. In His word He says, *I will never leave thee, nor forsake thee* (Hebrews 13:5). He will always be by your side. I pray you come across loyal people in your lifetime. Whether you do or you don't, know God will be there for you. You can trust Him. Don't hold on to the hurt of those who betray your loyalty. They were never meant to keep it. There is only one who will never change.

And thou shalt love the Lord thy God with all thine heart,
and with all thy soul, and with all thy might.
(Deuteronomy 6:5)

Don't stay in offense to a person who mismanages loyalty. There is a reason they were untrustworthy. Consider that they may not be able to follow where God is leading you.

THE OUTRO

SACRIFICE IS A major part of loyalty. What you sacrifice willingly will come back to you tenfold. God blesses us when we pour into others' cups, but we can't pour if our own cup is empty. Fill yourself up first! Read His word from the moment you wake up. Talk nicely to yourself. Make decisions throughout the day that are going to allow you to be there for others and for yourself. If you know you can't operate on four hours of sleep, why would you stay up all night talking on the phone to your best guy friend who is going through rough times? Shoot him a text, get your rest, then take him to lunch the next day and treat him. That's still loyalty.

I thank God for my children as they have been reciprocating the same loyal energy I give to them right back to me. I thank God for those people in my life who I trust and know would be there for me through thick and thin. You may not have anybody at all who is loyal to you or for you to be loyal to. One thing is for certain: God will never turn on you. He's the most faithful, reliable, and undeniable being you'll ever know. Everything goes back to Him. Everything is from Him. Everything you give—loyalty, love, kindness—should be from Him. Kill off people-pleasing and harness the true, deep loyalty to yourself, God, and others. That puts a smile on your Heavenly Father's face.

THE AFFIRMATION

I commit to remaining steadfast and
faithful in my relationship with God
and others as I continue to speak life
into my own soul.

chapter xiv

DEATH

Through my dad's death, I started understanding the plan that I was chosen to complete.

Tashera Simmons

THE INTRO

DEATH. Many fear it, while others look forward to it. I can say I've never been a fan of it, but it will meet me one day whether I like it or not. When my father left this earth, I felt as if it was the beginning of really dying to myself. He was my confidant and wise spiritual mentor. With death comes loss and grief, but do know there's something warm and bright on the other side of it all. Life after death is something we can aim toward, hope for, and look forward to. But what about death when it's right in front of you threatening your loved ones and sweeping through cities?

In many eulogies, you hear about turning sorrow and mourning into celebration and joy. At the time of my father's death, I thought, *"To hell with that. What is there to be happy for?"* I'm sure many of you may have felt the same when you lost someone you cared for. Maybe you were angry at God. I'm here to let you know you should embrace all those feelings. Feel them real good. The moment will pass, maybe not soon, but it will pass. Don't rush it or you may find yourself resorting to unhealthy habits like I did. Feel everything. Feel what it's like to be human. Death in all our humanity is a reality, while death to self is a spirituality that activates something within each of us.

THE STORY

OVER A YEAR AGO, I sat in a sterile and cold hospital waiting room with my eyes shut. I prayed to God for His healing and intervention for my dad who was upstairs in his hospital bed. He had cancer and had been sick for some time without telling any of his children. I knew God is a God of miracles. He had done so many before me that I just knew He would be able to pull this one off too. I opened my eyes and felt settled. The woman who had been conversing with me since the moment I got in the waiting room had a smile on her face. I watched her excitement bring her out of her seat.

At that same moment, my cousin Michelle called me on the phone. She let me know that my father went home to be with the Lord. My heart sank as I hung up the phone. As I struggled to get up and gather myself, the woman came over to me with the biggest smile.

"My daughter-in-law just had her baby! Our baby girl is here!" she said to me.

She had no idea that my father had been on the brink of death, so I genuinely responded by saying, "Congratulations!"

Her family began crowding around. There was so much going on at one time, like the flooding of a football after the playoffs. So much movement and excitement, yet I stood still. I've always heard the saying about when one goes, another comes in. We knew he was going, we just didn't know when. The grief was immediate and impacted my daily life.

I could barely get out of the bed in the mornings and when I did, I moved slowly and sluggishly doing everything I could with my mind set on getting back in bed. I felt as if I wasn't even living. His death made me feel as if I was dying myself. I just shut down. It was like cutting the power supply on a breaker. It all went down. I had a friend who I would speak to and a lot of people would check on me but whenever I would speak to anybody about my dad, I would cry. I never really cried like that. I would always try to stay strong. I allowed myself to be vulnerable in my father's death and cried for six months off and on, up and down.

His words stuck in my head. Almost everything he ever said would be playing on repeat, and I couldn't shake it.

"Daughter, much is given, much is received, much is required," he would say to me.

I would listen to him just as I used to when I was a little girl in Yonkers before his drug and alcohol abuse, before Earl, before my kids. It was me and him looking at trains going to concerts, talking the whole way home. In his last few years, I saw a metamorphosis take place, and he was the best dad I could have ever asked for.

"You are the one," he would always say.

That would aggravate my soul because I would think, "What does that even have to do with anything? What do you mean 'I'm the one?'" He would say that even when I was going through my divorce. When

I was in bed one day crying to myself, I understood what he meant. My father would have never wanted me to be in this fetal position not doing anything, not being productive.

He had said, "You're the one—the one that God chose."

He would always use the story of Job and ingrained in me everything I could ever learn from that biblical chapter. Through my dad's death, I started understanding the plan for which I was chosen. He used to always say, "Many are called, very few are chosen." He was so right.

When people would call me during that time, for some reason they wanted to talk about things going on in the world. I guess they were just calling to talk even though I know they were trying to support me. The way my mind was at the time, I wasn't suited to listen about the new headlines on stupid social media. It was best to send a text and say "I'm thinking about you. I'm praying for you" and that's it. I've since learned to do that when people are going through bereavement because there is nothing else to say.

To be totally honest, my relationship with death was nonexistent even though my ex-husband had passed on. There were times where I thought Earl didn't even want to live. With my dad, I just felt like death knocked on my door and it shook my whole home and shouted to everyone inside, "We're not going to be here forever!"

I heard death loud and clear. He needn't yell so dang loud, for my ears were ringing with truth. I had to tighten up. I remember thinking how moving forward choices that I make need to be solid. I need to be more true to myself and stop allowing people to take advantage of me. I need to live my life fully and be who God has called me to be!

My father used to always tell me to take care of myself and to be my best self. Yes, he had a bunch of issues growing up. I saw him do a lot of things that I just didn't approve of, but he dedicated the rest of his life after getting clean to me, my children, and his family. When I say family, I mean all his family and all his children even though he lived with me and my kids. So we got a lot of him, and he never did anything for himself. For him, he thought that was everything.

He would constantly show gratitude and say, "You've done good by me."

He was so blessed to have the life he did by the end given how he was raised and the different things he went through. I'm so grateful to God for instilling in me a heart of gold that enabled me to reconnect with my dad. I was able to fulfill all his traveling dreams! He was able to travel the world with me and my children and at special moments, he would look at me and say, "Thank you daughter." No one can ever take away from me those precious memories.

His past was what he was standing on, but he had a new outlook on life with a sober mind and a focus on his grandkids. It's like he finally got clean after losing so much of his life that he couldn't get back. He dedicated to us what time was left. All of this really simmered in my spirit and I thought, *"I need to get it together because he told me who I was, and now I know who I am. I need to be that person for my children and for myself!"*

I don't want to have any regrets in life. My children are my everything, just like my dad felt, but we differ in that I intend on doing things for myself as well. He went so long without doing that. I feel as if he thought he had to make up for it in the end. God didn't create us to just die. We have to live for Him and for ourselves. Dying to myself actually made me want to live even more. I had always been afraid of death and the unknown, remaining distant from it. At funerals, I wouldn't even step in to see the body. We all will die, yes, but what we do while we are here is pertinent.

THE LESSON

DYING TO YOURSELF is one of the hardest things to do. You have lived a life full of what you think you should do. Let me break it down for you.

We all die to ourselves.

You have to die to who you think you should be. We are born and told in school the different career paths to take. Since elementary school, you have told everyone you would be a lawyer. You watched shows and movies about the law and even read a few books. One day you are in high school and everything becomes real. You will graduate and you realize you don't want to be a lawyer. You have kept this up for so long but now you have discovered a love for all things cosmetology. The problem is, you don't want to let down the people who have dreamed of the day you would be in court with your first case. You are skilled enough for law school but not interested at all. You have to die to the part of yourself that only wants to follow a path because it's what you told everyone else. You have to submit to the part of you who knows cosmetology is your purpose. You look back and realize you were doing your doll's hair at 5 years old and all your friend's hair at 16 years old. God's purpose is for you to cure a scalp condition and He put that desire in your heart.

When you are always living life in a routine, you ignore the supernatural nudging.

Don't waste your days not doing what you were put here to do. It may not be a huge thing such as being on television. You may be the person who feeds the homeless at the local community center. When you consume all your time with mindless activities and sleep the rest of the day away, you are missing out. There are so many amazing things God has for your life. You have to die to the normal routine of life. Try to drive another way or book the getaway you have been putting off. Life is more than your living room and neighborhood. You have to die to the life of only your bills and issues. There is a huge world God wants you to impact.

The person God designed you to be is locked on the other side of the door you won't open.

To die to your flesh is a process. It takes God. You are not able to do it as an individual. It is a transformation. Think of a butterfly. It is a caterpillar first. It transitions into a beautiful creature but the truth is, it was beautiful to start with. The transition only brought forth what was on the inside. That is what God is doing when we die to ourselves. When we sacrifice and push our plates aside, we are letting God know we are ready. We open our bibles and read His thoughts, advice, wisdom, and stories, and let Him know we are ready to hear His voice and follow His steps. Your transformation begins when you decide to let God in.

Dying is a transition that's going to happen. It's inevitable.

The best way to understand this truth is to think of Jesus dying on the cross for our sins. He lived a short life filled with miracles, signs, and wonders. He did what he was purposed to do. He taught us about God and how to trust Him. He healed the sick, raised the dead, and fed the hungry, to name a few miracles. After all the good He did on this earth, there were still people who hated Him and betrayed Him. Their allegiance to the world caused Him to be tortured and placed on the cross. He transitioned to be with God. The plan of His death had to happen so that we could have life. We all have to pass on one day, but the way we live is how we are remembered. You have to die to your pride and humble yourself. You have to die to who the world told you to be and evolve into the person God called you to be.

And about the ninth hour Jesus cried with a loud voice, saying,
Eli, Eli, lama sabachthani? That is to say, "My God, my God, why
hast thou forsaken me?" (Matthew 27:46)

Jesus even died to Himself. He thought He was forsaken because His flesh was dying. He had to die to His own feelings in a moment bigger than Him. When He allowed God to work, He paved the way for us to be forgiven for our sins and have life.

196

THE OUTRO

IT'S IMPORTANT TO try to die to ourselves and live in the spirit. While we're here, there is something about dying to ourselves that changes everything. You can keep searching for love in all the wrong places, feeding yourself toxic spirits that prevent you from walking in purpose. You can do all these things that God never intended in an effort to feel content. What you can't do is all these things while dying to yourself. Those things have to experience a supernatural death so you can be alive spiritually again. That, my friends, will go far beyond contentment. With that comes joy and peace in the Holy Spirit.

Grief in my life from my ex-husband and my father has had an impact on me as a woman of God, but I never let it stop me from all the living there is left to do. Wherever you are in your journey—whether you're reading this book and by now are deciding you want to begin the process of dying to self or you realize you've already been doing it—remember that death is not where it ends. There's life after where you will be rewarded for your faithfulness to your Heavenly Father. I often think of a lyric from a gospel song that says, *"Right before I live, I have to die."* That's nothing but the truth.

THE AFFIRMATION

I am not afraid of death, as the hope
for eternal life allows me to rest in
the Father and continue His kingdom
work for the rest of my days.

chapter xv

EVERYTHING

When I say everything I give to Him,
I mean my finances, my love life,
and my children.

Tashera Simmons

THE INTRO

HAVE YOU EVER lost a $20 bill? How about $100? How did you feel? Did you just shrug your shoulders and go on? Nine times out of 10, you got a little aggravated. You searched and searched for it. In that moment, you lost something. It may never find its way back to you or maybe it will. If you lost everything you've ever worked for or was born into—family, friends, money, your home—would you curse God or would you still glorify Him?

I've had some reasons to curse God. I could've done it when my mother left. I could have done it when my father basically abandoned his family for drugs and alcohol. And I could have done it when my husband was unfaithful. We have to remember to glorify God in all we do regardless of how bad it seems. When you die to yourself, you have no issue with everything being so called "taken away" because there's a level of trust with God that everything is going to be okay.

THE STORY

A FAMILY MEMBER of mine went to Pastor Hazel with some major concerns years ago.

"She's lost it," he said to her, referring to me. "She's about to lose her house and everything, but here she is going around all happy-go-lucky. She doesn't have any money. She has lost it. I'm telling you. You're the only one that can get through to her."

"No, what you are witnessing is the peace that surpasses all human understanding," she said to him.

When pastor told me about this situation, I laughed to myself because only people who have truly felt this kind of peace can understand. Sometimes I don't even understand this peace. Even when I was about to lose my house, I was still blessed. I've always been blessed, and it has nothing to do with what I did. It has everything to do with God. I just gave Him everything because He has given me everything. The reciprocity of it is effortless. The Holy Spirit has truly taken residence in my soul. It came to a point where I fed my soul so much that this Holy Spirit came in, and He's been in control since.

I realized that nothing is really mine. What I used to think was mine has been God's all along. Nothing truly belongs to us, therefore, we should be giving Him everything that we claim to be our own. If we as humans take a second and think about where we really are on this planet, we'll see that we are tiny specks. We are in the middle of a dark universe with billions of different stars and surrounding galaxies. Because we wake up and see sun, rain, snow, or whatever luxuries that this planet has offered us, we have gotten too comfortable and take things for granted.

I can't control when the enemy attacks everything God has given me. I can't control when other people gossip behind my back and smile to my face. The only thing I have control of is how I conduct my peace, how I create my space, and how I think. I can't even control when God turns this vessel to dust and takes my spirit home. While I'm in this vessel, I have the power to think, create my own narrative of life, and keep my sanity. But everything else? Who knows. I don't know what's going to happen tomorrow. I have no idea. I could plan for tomorrow, but life may throw some curveballs that come unexpectedly. I still have to find a way to knock them out of the park.

He's omnipotent and omnipresent. He knew from the time I was a kid that my mother would leave. He knew that I would become a young mother overnight. He knew I would go through a divorce. He knew that to many it would appear as if I had lost everything at one point in my life but despite how things appeared, not a single thing was lost. The enemy did not win even though it felt as if he knew my triggers. It's as if he knew where to hurt me, and he constantly stayed there. It was as if history just kept repeating itself in my life. Abandonment and betrayal just continued. The constant cycle of it kept spinning and spinning. I would ask God, "What are you trying to tell me because I have not shattered yet?" It surprises me that I did not end up in a psychiatric ward after the different storms that I've gone through. But God.

Now at 53, I'm like, "God I am giving you everything because I realize that I cannot do life without you. I need to be on point. I need to be more disciplined and intentional when I pray. I need to come to you like my Father. How do I move in this next season? What do you want from me? What do you want me to do? How do you want me to do this? This life isn't about me any more. It's all about you because you have been there."

When I say everything I give to Him, I mean my finances, my love life, and my children. When you give your children to God, there's no worry. Giving my kids to God was huge because as parents, we feel that we have to have our hands on our kids and be in their lives at all times. Early on before I gave everything of myself to God, I found that I couldn't do it all. He is everything and is everywhere. I'm only this little person but if I give all of my trust to Him, He will see to the well-being of my kids. It's really letting go and letting God. He goes before us because it says in the bible that we have a choice. He will never just come in and take over like a bulldozer plowing through raw materials, taking up space unannounced and uninvited. He is going to give you a choice. You have to let Him in. When you make the choice, He comes in like a gentleman and orchestrates your life so elegantly. It's as if He's planning and plotting this beautiful, glossy, yellow-brick-road full of all the jewels and the milk and honey talked about in the word. He's a gracious God whether we give Him everything or not.

I think about the story of Job. The devil thought that Job, who was a man of great wealth and many blessings in life, would curse God if He were to take it all away. God took the devil up on this challenge. He knew His son would not falter. He put it all to the test and let the devil take whatever he wanted from Job. But there was a limit to what he could do, for the devil could not take Job's life. Job never broke. Even when the devil took his children, he didn't break. There were times where I felt like Job. The devil covered him with blisters and he hurt. I haven't been covered in blisters, but I've felt the psychological pain of a thousand blisters in my mind. I've had my closest family members say, "Why do you even trust God after that? How do you even believe in Him? How do you even go to church?" And the answer is always the same: "I just give my all to Him."

I'm not saying that life gets easier just because you give Him your all. Trials still come but just knowing that you have God taking care of every single battle, every single warfare gives you a sense of peace. It's peace I never witnessed in my life but I've finally gotten there. I was able to get there by dying to myself.

THE LESSON

GIVING GOD EVERYTHING is easier said than done. When you are on top, you don't want to let go. Looking up from the bottom, you may feel you have nothing to give. Let me help you out.

Don't make this world your god.

God makes it very clear who He is saying, "I am that I am." When you start to make things your god, you allow them to become your idols. Exodus 17:20 tells us, *Thou shalt have no other gods before me.* When you put your job, children, business, or relationships first, you are making the world your god. Elevation and success to us is not defined the same way by God. You can compromise yourself striving for an opportunity that God doesn't even want you to have. It will knock you out of the position He placed you in for the place you want to be. Think about the time you were going to open up your bible and read it but then changed your mind because you had work to do. What about when you started to pray and your phone rang. Once you hung up the line you forgot all about praying and went on with your day. Those small things start the downward spiral of placing God on the back burner and the world in the forefront.

Spend time with God.

Time doesn't last forever. We adjust our lives to Daylight Savings Time but not for God. Spending time with Him in prayer and worship is everything. Give Him the first words from your lips in the morning. Sing songs that give Him thanks and gratitude. Don't confine yourself to only speaking to God in a religious setting. You can spend time with Him in your car on the way to work, at the park with your kids, on your walk, and when you're exercising. This list could go on and on. Don't limit yourself because God has no limits. He hears you wherever you are.

Everything is from God.

The air you breathe, the clothes on your back, and the shoes on your feet come from God. Let's take it a step further: The ground you walk on is from God. How can you not give Him everything? It came from Him to you. God is creation. When God tells me to give something away, I don't get sad because He gave it to me. When your home gets foreclosed on or your car repossessed, just know God has more for you. He gave you the house and the car. If He is allowing it to be taken away, it's for a reason. He may want you to move to a better neighborhood with more support for your family. There may be a storm coming that will wipe out everything two years from now and the only way to get you to move is to take it from you. There are times where we are in

God's way because we are tied to material things. This is why He wants you to stay close to Him because He will let you know when time is up. It's time for a new level. Think of holding on to the small toy as a child. You broke it so the sound doesn't work, but it was your favorite. God has the new and improved version when you finally throw the old one away. Don't be afraid to give up your things. Just as He gave you the old, He will give you the new.

God is everything.

If you really look at it, this world is nothing but an illusion because it's temporary. God has given us a world full of all His creations and beautiful things. He didn't do that for us to worship them but to glorify Him. He is the maker of all those things. We find ourselves thanking people more than God. He sent us those people to assist us with His plan. They would have never come around if we didn't need help. God sends us resources in the form of people, places, and things to accomplish our purpose for Him on this earth. He makes the sun shine, rain fall, and flowers grow. I could go on and on. He is in the molecules of your DNA. God is everything. He is in everything. Without Him, nothing would exist. There is no need to cry over what you have lost in life or have yet to gain because with Him and in Him you have everything you could possibly need. God is not on our time but stands outside of time. He is everything, in every moment, of everyday.

And we know that all things work together for good to them that love God, to them who are the called according to his purpose.
(Romans 8:28)

I always quote this scripture because it's true everyday. Whenever you feel down and out, pick yourself up and know that all things work together. Everything happens for a reason.

THE OUTRO

WHEN YOU GIVE God everything, die to your flesh, and live in the Spirit, it's the best place that you can ever be while you're living in this life. But you must die to yourself. The term "dying" often has a negative connotation, as if it is this bad thing. Dying is transition. It's progress from something that proceeded to live. A lot of behaviors and traits that are rooted in trauma, hurt, and attacks from the enemy need to die. They aren't serving you any good. You have the power to make it happen, and you have the tools.

Don't quit because it gets hard. There are so many people who give up on life because they can't do the simple act of giving God everything—their hurts, pains, and trials. They don't belong to you anyway. There's this false ownership as if we aren't God's creation and aren't His and His alone. Let that stuff die. Let your old self die, and make God your everything.

THE AFFIRMATION

Everything I have is a gift from God.
I give it all back to Him in faith and
obedience.

conclusion

DESPITE ALL MY hesitations about writing this book, I was able to shake off the nerves and get it done by surrendering to the Holy Spirit. Surrender is more than just a word. It's probably one of the hardest things to do, especially if you have trust issues, trauma, grudges, and are holding on to something. Surrendering is letting go and trusting that it will all be okay. It is not giving up the fight but rather knowing that the outcome of the battle is in your favor. It's the relaxing, unclenching, and easing of the soul—the self-soothing after hugging yourself too tightly during a lifetime of heartbreak and hardship.

When you do surrender in spirit, all the things God tried telling you before come back to the surface. He shows Himself strong in many ways that are not to be ignored. The more you ignore the tugging and nudging of the Holy Spirit, the further you are from what you are destined to become and do. When you die to yourself, that nudging and tugging is so strong that you have no choice but to obey and listen to what God has to tell you.

For so long, the pain in my flesh cut so deep. If my spiritual man had not come alive, I don't know where I would be mentally today. I know I wouldn't be the resilient, caring, and loving person that I've blossomed into these past few years. My prayer life, being consistent in all that I do, and constantly feeding my spirit are some ways I remain balanced. As days and weeks pass, my spiritual life grows. There are no days off if I want to maintain this equilibrium, for the wicked schemes of the enemy are always at hand.

As far as specific practices that have helped me, gratitude comes to mind as well as being intentional in my thinking and what I pray for. If I find myself slipping to a depressive episode due to the spirit of comparison, I have to be intentional about what I expose myself to. My thought patterns are impressionable and sometimes social media is such a distraction. I've recently found myself face buried in my phone screen before realizing it distracts me so much hours on end. What wasted time and energy!

At the beginning of the day, the first thing I do is say, "Thank you Jesus for waking me up." Every day I can wake up and take control of the day. I can decide how I will react to situations. Me. Tashera. No one else can decide for me. There is something about being intentional. Starting my day like this gives me a feeling of peace. As I have shared in this book, I've been in the eye of the storm and spiritually under warfare, but I was never standing alone in the midst of it all.

Having a routine and spiritual practice has proved beyond helpful, including reading scripture and going to church. I must feed my spirit before I feed my flesh. In fact, the more my flesh starves, the more spiritually hungry I become. That hunger lies in a desire to know Jesus and to experience His comfort. He's always walked close to me, I've just sometimes been too much in my flesh to see it.

I may have laid to rest all the parts of me that kept me from what others would consider to be a prosperous path but sure enough, I'm very much alive. When I died to myself, Christ resurrected me as a new creature of His making. Because of this, I am a better mother, a better daughter, a better human being. I'm so thankful for everything the Lord threw my way because it made me who I am today. I'm far from perfect, but I'm living life as I was meant to now. Writing this book has brought me healing, and I hope it serves as the first step toward your own.

Is dying to yourself fun? No. Absolutely not. Is paying your bills something you look forward to every month? No, but you do it anyway! You do it so you don't have to move around in darkness. Having the convenience of flipping a switch to light up your hallway can make all the difference in the world. You do it so you have a roof over your head. I understand what it is like to go without and that sometimes, paying bills isn't as easy as I'm making it sound. Stay with me here.

Let's say money isn't an issue. Your light bill comes in the mail. You have the choice to either get your card out and make a payment or to spend it on a fun night out with the family. Let's say you choose to go to a fancy dinner with your family and then go see the newest movie right after. When you come home and flip the switch in the foyer, nothing. Darkness. Boy, do they work fast! The choice between doing something you needed to do versus doing something you wanted to do ultimately led to a result that ended in inconvenience. There was nothing wrong with having fun with family but because of that decision, you and your family were not ready for the darkness that met you when you came home.

My point is, you may not be ready to die to yourself, and that's okay. If you decide to go out on faith and begin the process, you'll be better equipped against certain attacks of the enemy versus someone who is still very much in their flesh. I'm challenging you, dear reader, to make a choice. Are you going to live in the sin you so comfortably swim in every day? Or are you going to step out of the pool a better version of yourself, stand in the light, and clothe yourself in the armor of God?

By no means is John 3:16 an overused staple of the Christian faith. It is the blueprint. It reads: *For God so loved the world, that he gave his only begotten Son, that whoever believes in him shall not perish but have eternal life.* God loves you just as much as He loves me. I don't know about you, but eternal life sounds like the real prize. While we're here on earth, we should make our Heavenly Father proud. We do things that anger and disappoint Him, but all is forgiven when we repent. Whether you are going through a messy divorce, chemo treatments, or struggling to make ends meet, know that there is a God who loves you enough to send His own son to die for you. That is truly awesome.

The question is, what are you willing to die for? More importantly, are you willing to let your old sinful habits die? Are you willing to die to self? Whatever your answer may be, know that life truly begins when your sinful behavior ends.

about the author

TASHERA SIMMONS is a woman who has turned life's toughest trials into her most powerful triumphs. Tashera's life is a remarkable "rags to riches" story that began in Yonkers, New York, where she faced obstacles that would break many. At just 11 years old, she met the late hip-hop icon **DMX**. Their connection profoundly shaped their lives. An entrepreneur, author, motivational speaker, and devoted mother of four, Tashera embodies resilience, courage, and an unwavering commitment to uplifting others. Known for her warmth, authenticity, and transformative storytelling, she is a beacon of hope for those navigating life's hardest challenges. Actively working with organizations such as the YWCA and Young Life, Tashera is also the founder of her newly launched 501(c)(3) nonprofit, *My Freedom Project Foundation*, which is dedicated to empowering youth through financial literacy, credit education, and comprehensive mental health support. Tashera has learned three powerful truths through her life journey: Trauma is universal, happiness is a choice, and faith can carry you through anything.

As she steps into the next chapter of her life, Tashera is expanding her reach as an author, following the release of her first book, *You Think You Know, but You Have No Idea.* She is also a speaker, and an advocate. Her story is one of survival and transformation, offering a message of hope and resilience to all who hear it. With her sights set on inspiring others to embrace their strength, find joy amidst challenges, and create lives rooted in faith and purpose, **Tashera Simmons** is redefining what it means to rise with grace, gratitude, and a fearless love for life.

CONNECT WITH TASHERA SIMMONS

Instagram	@Tasherasimmons
Facebook	@Tasherasimmons
Threads	@Tasherasimmons
Snapchat	@Tasherasimmons